ADULT READING SERIES

CHALLENGER

TEACHER'S MANUAL

FOR BOOK 7

COREA MURPHY

ISBN 0-88336-794-7

© 1988

New Readers Press
Publishing Division of Laubach Literacy International
Box 131, Syracuse, New York 13210

Printed in the United States of America

Cover design by Chris Steenwerth

9 8 7 6 5 4

About the Author

Corea Murphy has worked in the field of education since the early 1960s. In addition to classroom and tutorial teaching, Ms. Murphy has developed language arts curriculum guides for public high schools, conducted curriculum and effectiveness workshops, and established an educational program for residents in a drug rehabilitation facility.

Ms. Murphy became interested in creating a reading series for older students when she began working with adults and adolescents in the early 1970s. The **Challenger Adult Reading Series** is the result of her work with these students.

In a very real sense, the students contributed greatly to the development of this reading series. Their enthusiasm for learning to read and their willingness to work hard provided inspiration, and their many helpful suggestions influenced the content of both the student books and the teacher's manuals.

It is to these students that the **Challenger Adult Reading Series** is dedicated with the hope that others who wish to become good readers will find this reading program both helpful and stimulating.

A special note of gratitude is also extended to Kay Koschnick, Christina Jagger, and Mary Hutchison of New Readers Press for their work and support in guiding this series to completion.

Table of Contents

Introduction to the *Challenger* Series

The *Challenger Adult Reading Series* is a program designed to develop reading, writing, and reasoning skills in adult and adolescent students. The first four books in the *Challenger* series emphasize *learning to read*, developing basic decoding, vocabulary, comprehension, and writing skills. Beginning with Book 5, the emphasis shifts to *reading to learn*, developing higher-level comprehension and reasoning skills while expanding the student's knowledge base.

Components of the Series

The *Challenger* series contains:
- 8 student books
- 5 teacher's manuals
- answer keys for Books 1–4 and 5–8
- the *Challenger Placement Tool*
- 8 puzzle books correlated to the student books
- 4 books of writing activities correlated to Books 1–4

The Student Books

Each book in this controlled vocabulary series contains 20 lessons, plus reviews. Each lesson includes:
- word study
- a reading selection
- a wide variety of exercises and activities

In Books 1, 3, 5, and 7, each lesson begins with a word chart that introduces new words according to specific phonics principles. In all books, new words that appear in the lesson are listed before each reading selection.

The reading selections in the odd-numbered books are mostly fiction. Books 1 and 3 contain original stories about a group of adults in a variety of situations. Most reading selections in Books 5 and 7 are minimally adapted well-known works of fiction. The even-numbered books contain engaging informational readings. The selections in Books 2 and 4 are on topics similar to those in magazines and encyclopedias. Most selections in Books 6 and 8 are adapted from highly respected works of nonfiction that enable students to broaden the scope of their knowledge.

The varied exercises and activities help students to develop their reading, writing, speaking, and listening skills and to increase their basic knowledge. Comprehension exercises based on the reading selections focus on the development of literal, inferential, and applied comprehension skills. In addition, comprehension exercises in Books 5 through 8 develop literary understanding, interpretation, and critical reading skills.

Other exercises are designed to increase vocabulary and develop reading and reasoning skills. They include vocabulary reviews; word associations; classifying, sequencing, and categorizing exercises; using context clues; forming analogies; using dictionaries and reference materials; and several types of puzzles.

There are reviews after every four or five lessons, except in Books 1 and 3. Each book has a final review. Also included in Books 1 through 5 are indexes of the words introduced so far in that book. The word indexes for Books 6 through 8 are included in the teacher's manuals. These word indexes can be used in developing reinforcement activities and vocabulary reviews.

The Teacher's Manuals

There is a single *Teacher's Manual for Books 1–4* and individual teacher's manuals for Books 5, 6, 7, and 8. These comprehensive manuals explain the concepts underlying the *Challenger* series and offer practical suggestions about procedures and techniques for working with students. Separate chapters deal with preparing to teach, teaching the lessons, writing, reinforcement activities, and using the lesson notes. These chapters should be read before you begin to use this program. Individual lesson notes containing suggestions for pre-reading, post-reading, and writing activities, and comments on specific exercises should be read before teaching the lessons. In the teacher's manuals, there are also introductions to each book, scope and sequence charts, and answer keys for each book. Finally, the *Teacher's Manual for Books 1–4* contains a chart of the common phonics principles and elements in English words.

Student Writing

Students are encouraged to write from the very first lesson. Early in the series, exercises focus on writing at the sentence level and are designed to simultaneously improve spelling, sentence structure, and students' skill in expressing themselves clearly. Most lessons in Books 5 through 8 have exercises that require students to write brief paragraphs. Suggestions for providing additional writing activities are given in the individual lesson notes.

Significant Educational Features

Flexibility and Adaptability

The *Challenger* series has been successfully with students in many different types of instructional settings:

- adult volunteer literacy programs
- ABE, pre-GED, and GED programs
- secondary remedial reading programs
- secondary special education programs
- community college reading programs
- educational programs in correctional institutions
- workforce tutorial programs for employees

Challenger can be used in one-to-one tutoring situations, as well as in a variety of group settings. The lessons can be adapted to fit a variety of formats, allowing you to introduce additional activities and topics related to individual student interests and needs.

An Integrated Approach

Challenger integrates reading, writing, speaking, and listening skills. Reading comprehension is developed through oral discussion of inferential- and applied-level questions. These discussions help students to develop speaking and listening skills. Students build writing skills through follow-up writing activities. Critical thinking and reasoning skills are developed as students discuss the readings, the exercises, and their writing activities.

Sequenced Skill Building

Each lesson builds upon the skills developed and the content introduced in previous lessons. Students are continually challenged as the lessons increase in length and difficulty. As reading selections become longer, the content, vocabulary, and sentence structure become more sophisticated and demanding. The exercises and writing activities build on and expand students' knowledge and abilities. Students experience a sense of progress as they learn to apply their skills to new situations.

Highly Motivating Material

Students who have used the *Challenger* series have commented that this reading program has many characteristics that help to hold their interest and maintain their motivation. The characteristics they most frequently cite include:

- exceptionally motivating reading selections
- mature and diverse material
- information that increases background knowledge
- emphasis on using reasoning powers
- challenge of increasingly difficult materials
- feelings of success and confidence generated by the program

Placement

The *Challenger Placement Tool*, used in conjunction with information you have about a student's background knowledge, speaking and writing abilities, and motivation, can help you to decide where to place the student in the *Challenger* series. Scores on standardized reading inventories can also be used. For the first four books, scores in the following reading level ranges are appropriate:

Book 1: 2.0	**Book 3:** 3.0–4.5
Book 2: 2.0–3.0	**Book 4:** 4.0–5.0

Keep in mind that numerical reading levels by themselves are not adequate descriptors of adult reading abilities. For students already using the series, scoring 85 per cent or better on the final review in each book indicates that the student is ready to go on to the next book.

Although it is recognized that there are students of both sexes, for the sake of clarity and simplicity, we chose to use the pronouns *he, him,* and *his* throughout this book.

SCOPE AND SEQUENCE: BOOK 7

Lesson	1	2	3	4	R	5	6	7	8	R	9	10	11	12	R	13	14	15	16	R	17	18	19	20	R
Word Analysis																									
1. Use phonics and syllabication skills to decode words	☆	☆	☆	☆	☆	☆	☆	☆	☆	☆	☆	☆	☆	☆	☆	☆	☆	☆	☆	☆	☆	☆	☆	☆	☆
2. Review basic phonics sounds/patterns	☆	☆	☆			☆														★			☆	☆	
3. Recognize/use word families				★	★					★				☆			☆	☆		★					
4. Use homonyms correctly	☆				★										★		★								★
Vocabulary																									
1. Learn unfamiliar vocabulary	★	★	★	★	★	★	★	★	★	★	★	★	★	★	★	★	★	★	★	★	★	★	★	★	★
2. Infer word meanings from context clues	★	★	★	★	★	★	★	★	★	★	★	★	★	★	★	★	★	★	★	★	★	★	★	★	★
3. Identify definitions/descriptions of terms	★	★	★	★	★	★	★	★	★	★	★	★	★	★	★	★	★	★	★	★	★	★	★	★	★
4. Learn/use rules pertaining to standard English usage	☆				★	★									★		★							★	
5. Complete word associations			★	★	★											★							★		
6. Identify synonyms																★							★		
7. Identify antonyms				★	★	★	★									★							★		
8. Learn common affixes and roots:																									
-al				☆					☆																
-ly													☆												
-ness																☆									
-ist																	☆					☆			
uni-																						☆			
bi-																						☆			
tri-																									
cred	☆				★	★																		★	★
9. Complete analogies	☆	☆			☆						☆							☆	☆			☆		☆	
10. Learn/review idioms, sayings, and proverbs			☆	☆					☆	☆		☆		★	★			☆				☆			★
11. Complete word puzzles																									
Comprehension																									
1. Identify words using context clues	★	★	★	★	★	★	★	★	★	★	★	★	★	★	★	★	★	★	★	★	★	★	★	★	★
2. Read selections independently	★	★	★	★	★	★	★	★	★	★	★	★	★	★	★	★	★	★	★	★	★	★	★	★	★
3. Complete exercises independently	★	★	★	★	★	★	★	★	★	★	★	★	★	★	★	★	★	★	★	★	★	★	★	★	★
4. Improve listening comprehension	☆	☆	☆	☆	☆	☆	☆	☆	☆	☆	☆	☆	☆	☆	☆	☆	☆	☆	☆	☆	☆	☆	☆	☆	☆
5. Improve oral reading	☆	☆	☆	☆	☆	☆	☆	☆	☆	☆	☆	☆	☆	☆	☆	☆	☆	☆	☆	☆	☆	☆	☆	☆	☆
6. Develop literal comprehension skills:																									
- Recall details	★	★	★	★	★	★	★	★	★	★	★	★	★	★	★	★	★	★	★	★	★	★	★	★	★
- Locate specific information	★	★	★	★	★	★	★	★	★	★	★	★	★	★	★	★	★	★	★	★	★	★	★	★	★
- Recall or establish sequence of events				☆																	☆				

Key: ★ = Primary emphasis   ☆ = Secondary emphasis   ☆ = Integrated with other skills

Comprehension, cont.

Lesson	1	2	3	4	R	5	6	7	8	R	9	10	11	12	R	13	14	15	16	R	17	18	19	20	R
7. Develop inferential comprehension skills:																									
- Support statements with appropriate details	★	★	★	★	★	★	★	★	★	★	★		★	★	★	★		★	★	★	★	★	★	★	
- Infer word meanings from context clues	★	★	★	★	★	★	★	★	★	★	★	★	★	★	★	★	★	★	★	★	★	★	★	★	★
- Infer information from the reading or exercises	★	★	★	★	★	★	★	★	★	★	★	★	★	★	★	★	★	★	★	★	★	★	★	★	★
- Use context clues to fill in missing words	★	★		★	★																				
- Draw conclusions based on reading	★			★	★	★	★	★	★	★	★	★	★	★	★	★	☆	☆	★	★	☆	★	☆	★	★
- Identify/infer cause & effect relationships	☆	☆	☆	☆	☆	☆	☆	☆	☆		☆	☆	☆	☆	☆	☆	☆	☆	☆	★	☆	☆	☆	☆	☆
- Classify words under topic headings					☆	☆	☆	☆												☆	☆	☆	☆		
- Identify tone of voice														★											
8. Develop applied comprehension skills:																									
- Relate reading to personal experience	☆		☆		★	☆	☆	☆					☆		☆	☆	☆					★			
- Draw conclusions based on personal experience	☆	☆	☆		☆	☆	☆	☆					☆		☆								☆	☆	
9. Learn/review basic factual information	☆	☆	☆	☆	☆	☆	☆	☆	☆	☆	☆					☆	☆	☆	☆	☆	☆	☆	☆	☆	

Literary Understanding

Lesson	1	2	3	4	R	5	6	7	8	R	9	10	11	12	R	13	14	15	16	R	17	18	19	20	R
1. Identify/interpret characters' actions, motivations, feelings, and qualities	★	★	★	★	★	★	★	★	★		★	★	★	★	★	★	★	★	★	★	★		★	★	
2. Identify/interpret plot	★	★	★	★	★	★	★	★	★	★	★	★	★	★	★	★	★	★	★	★	★	★	★	★	
3. Infer attitudes/qualities of characters	☆	☆	☆	☆	☆	☆	☆	★	★		☆	☆	★	★	★	★	★	★	★		☆		☆	☆	
4. Relate to characters' motivations & feelings	★	★	★	★	☆	★	★	★	★				★	☆	☆	☆	☆	☆		☆	☆	★			
5. Distinguish between fiction & nonfiction	☆	☆	☆	☆				☆	☆	☆	☆	☆	☆		☆	☆	☆	☆		☆	☆	☆	☆	☆	
6. Relate sayings/concepts to reading	★		☆	★		★	★		★	★	☆			☆							★			★	
7. Infer/interpret author's purpose/attitude		☆			★	★			☆	☆			☆	☆	☆					★	★				
8. Interpret poetry					★				☆	★		★	★	★	★				★	★			★	★	
9. Infer attitude of speaker in a poem					★				★	★			★	★	★				★						
10. Interpret figurative language	☆	☆			★		☆				★			★				★	★			★			
11. Predict outcome/aftermath of selection	☆					★																			
12. Identify theme of selection		☆				☆		☆	☆	☆	☆				☆										
13. Compare & contrast characters				★	☆	☆	☆	★		★	☆	☆	★	★	☆	☆	☆	★	★	★	☆			★	
14. Identify/interpret setting		☆	☆	☆		☆	☆	☆			☆	☆	★	★					☆		☆	☆	☆		
15. Describe personal reaction to reading	★			★	☆	★	☆	☆	☆		☆		★												
16. Recognize symbols					☆		☆					☆		☆	☆	★		★					☆	★	☆
17. Interpret drama																	★								
18. Recognize biography															☆										

Key: ★ = Primary emphasis   ☆ = Secondary emphasis   ☆ = Integrated with other skills

Writing

Lesson	1	2	3	4	R	5	6	7	8	R	9	10	11	12	R	13	14	15	16	R	17	18	19	20	R
1. Write sentence or paragraph answers to questions	★	★	★	★	★	★	★	★	★	★	☆	☆	★	★	★	★	★	★	★	★	★	★	★	★	★
2. Form a reasoned opinion	★	★	★	★	★	★	★	★	★	★	★	★	★	★	★	★	★	★	★	★	★	★	★	★	★
3. Copy words accurately	☆	☆	☆	☆	☆	☆	☆	☆	☆	☆	☆	☆	☆	☆	☆	☆	☆	☆	☆	☆	☆	☆	☆	☆	☆
4. Spelling:																									
- Spell words with greater accuracy	☆	☆	☆	☆	☆	☆	☆	☆	☆	☆	☆	☆	☆	☆	☆	☆	☆	☆	☆	☆	☆	☆	☆	☆	☆
- Identify misspelled words					★		☆					★													
- Change y to i before adding suffix								☆	☆																
- Recognize hyphenated words																			☆						

Note: Specific suggestions for additional writing assignments appear in the individual lesson notes and in Chapter 5 of this manual.

Study Skills

Lesson	1	2	3	4	R	5	6	7	8	R	9	10	11	12	R	13	14	15	16	R	17	18	19	20	R
1. Increase concentration	☆	☆	☆	☆	☆	☆	☆	☆	☆	☆	☆	☆	☆	☆	☆	☆	☆	☆	☆	☆	☆	☆	☆	☆	☆
2. Skim selection to locate information	☆	☆	☆	☆	☆	☆	☆	☆	☆	☆	☆	☆	☆	☆	☆	☆	☆	☆	☆	☆	☆	☆	☆	☆	☆
3. Apply reasoning skills to exercises:																									
- context clues	★	☆	☆	★	☆	☆	☆	☆	★	☆	★	★	★	☆	☆	★	☆	★	★	☆	★	★	☆	☆	☆
- process of elimination	☆	☆	☆	☆	☆	☆	☆	☆	☆	☆	☆	☆	☆	☆	☆	☆	☆	☆	☆	☆	☆	☆	☆	☆	☆
- "intelligent guessing"	☆	☆	☆	☆	☆	☆	☆	☆	☆	☆	☆	☆	☆	☆	☆	☆	☆	☆	☆	☆	☆	☆	☆	☆	☆
4. Use a dictionary:																									
- to look up word meanings	☆	☆	☆	☆	☆	☆	☆	☆	☆	☆	☆	☆	☆	☆	☆	☆	☆	☆	☆	☆	☆	☆	☆	☆	☆
- to learn word origins																							☆		
5. Use reference materials:																									
- to find factual/geographical information		☆		☆			☆	☆				☆				☆	☆						☆		
- to establish chronological order																									

1. Introduction to Book 7

The format of Book 7 corresponds to the one used in earlier odd-numbered books in the *Challenger* series. Each lesson begins with a word chart which introduces words into this controlled-vocabulary series according to specific phonics principles.

Definitions of difficult words from the word chart appear in a matching exercise which immediately follows each word chart. All students should own or have access to a dictionary in order to complete these exercises.

Most reading selections in Book 7 are minimally adapted from well-known and well-written literary pieces, such as short stories, folk tales, drama, and myths. Take time to point out to the students that they are reading quality literature. Experience indicates that students' self-esteem and motivation are bolstered when they realize that they are studying widely-acclaimed authors.

The exercises and reviews in Book 7 help the students further develop their comprehension skills, recall, and reasoning abilities. Literary understanding is emphasized in the reading comprehension exercises. In addition, material on standard English usage is introduced.

A review appears after every four lessons. These reviews provide students with additional opportunities to review words and concepts. They also help students develop the habit of referring to previous lessons for the correct answers to some of the questions.

Book 7 is the appropriate starting point for students who score in the 7.5-8.5 range on standardized reading achievement tests. The final review in Book 6 can also be used as a diagnostic tool. An accuracy rate of 85% or better for this review indicates that students are ready for Book 7.

Students who use this book should be given as many opportunities for oral reading practice as time permits. This practice helps to develop confidence, enjoyment, and interest in reading.

Book 7 builds upon procedures and practices emphasized in the earlier books in this series. Thus, you may find it worthwhile to look through the manual notes for some of these books.

Scheduling Considerations

Book 7 works well in a classroom setting. The most progress is achieved when students work with *Challenger* a minimum of 45 minutes two or three times a week. Students can work independently, in a group, or with a partner. When working with other students, they receive the support and stimulation from one another that makes learning more enjoyable. Also, the more advanced students can assume much of the responsibility for giving explanations and leading reinforcement activities, which in turn reinforces their own reading skills. Experience indicates that less advanced students usually benefit from peer instruction provided that you are available to supply any necessary clarifications.

The Lesson Components

Later chapters of this manual outline the principles and procedures that form the foundation of this reading series. The major components of the lessons in Book 7 are briefly described below.

Word Chart

Like the earlier odd-numbered books in this series, Book 7 uses common phonics principles to organize the introduction of new words. Words presented in this manner help students to understand better the many patterns that exist in the English language. This awareness, in turn, contributes to students' reading development. How much emphasis you place on the phonics principles reviewed in these word charts depends upon the spelling and pronunciation needs of your students.

Definitions

A matching exercise directly follows each word chart. Words in this exercise are taken from the word chart. Students are encouraged to use a dictionary for unfamiliar words. For this exercise, 100% accuracy is desired.

Words for Study

This section, which precedes the reading selection in each lesson, lists words in the lesson that appear for the first time in this series. As was the case in the earlier books, these words appear in the same order and form in which they initially appear in the lesson. This gives students additional practice in pronouncing word endings accurately.

Story

The readings for Book 7 have been organized into five units: Love and Money, Struggle, Courage, Brushes with Death, and Giving. It is important for students to understand that most of the readings are pieces of fiction rather than factual articles. The terms *fiction* and *nonfiction* can be introduced or reviewed. In addition to the adaptations of short stories, five other types of literature are presented: myth (Lesson 9), drama (Lessons 13, 19, 20), biography (Lesson 14), folktale (Lesson 17), and essay (Lesson 18).

All initial readings, with the exception of the first lesson, are to be done as homework.

About the Story

The comprehension questions call for a variety of different responses: multiple choice, fill-in-the-blank, and complete sentence responses. This variety gives students practice with formats that appear on both job-placement tests and the GED Test—two exams that many students using this book may well encounter.

Other Exercises

A wide variety of exercises has been included to help students improve their recall, increase their vocabulary, and develop their reasoning abilities. As often as seems appropriate, draw students' attention to the fact that reasoning is an essential part of reading. Help them develop such patterns as using the process of elimination, making intelligent guesses, using the dictionary, and referring to previous lessons when completing these exercises.

A score of 80% or higher should be considered satisfactory on these exercises. If students consistently score below this figure, take some time to help them pinpoint the problem. Generally, they are trying to complete the exercises too rapidly.

Because students are encouraged to learn from their mistakes, they should not be penalized for making them. If you work in a school which gives report cards, it is strongly recommended that evaluations be based on corrected work and overall progress rather than on students' initial efforts. In no way does this practice encourage typical reading students to be careless in completing their homework. Rather they usually become more interested in reading than in report cards, they are more relaxed and patient with themselves in completing assignments, and they develop a more realistic definition of academic progress.

Reinforcement Activities

Suggestions and procedures for reinforcement activities for those words and concepts that give students difficulty are discussed in Chapter 4.

Writing Assignments

Student writing is discussed in Chapter 5. It is recommended that students working in Book 7 complete weekly writing assignments of 250-500 words in addition to the writing that is required to complete the exercises in the individual lessons. Paragraphs or brief essays about discussion topics that interest students and personal and/or business letters are appropriate writing assignments. Suggestions for writing assignments are also given in the individual lesson notes.

The Lesson Format

The procedure for each lesson should be as consistent as possible.

1. Students go over the writing assignment if one was given and review the work in the previous lesson first. This includes discussing the reading selection and correcting the exercises.
2. If time permits, students complete relevant reinforcement activities. The nature and scope of these activities are determined by the needs of your students and how often you meet with them.
3. Students preview the next lesson, which is usually assigned for homework.

Individual Lesson Notes

Lesson notes for each individual lesson appear in Chapter 7 of this manual. These notes contain suggestions and procedures for specific items in each lesson.

Answer Key

An answer key for all the exercises in each lesson of Book 7 follows the individual lesson notes.

Word Indexes

The word indexes at the back of this manual contain lists of words that are introduced to this series in each unit of Book 7. There is also a master list of all the words introduced in this book. These lists are helpful when developing reinforcement activities. Students may also want to consult these lists periodically.

The next three chapters give suggestions for preparing and teaching the lessons and selecting reinforcement activities.

2. Preparing to Teach

The following suggestions are based on the author's experiences and those of other teachers who have used these books. You may find that your own situation renders some of these suggestions either impractical or impossible to implement in your classroom. It is hoped, however, that most of these suggestions can be modified to meet your particular needs.

How Often to Use *Challenger*

In general, it is recommended that teachers use *Challenger* with students two or three times a week for at least 45 minutes per session. If you meet five times a week with pre-GED students who are eager to pass the tests and have time outside the classroom to complete homework assignments, you may want to use *Challenger* every day.

If you meet five times a week with an adult or adolescent reading class that does not have a specific task such as GED preparation to motivate them, the recommended schedule is to focus on the lessons three times a week and devote the other two class sessions to activities which reinforce or enrich material presented in the lessons. Suggestions about these reinforcement activities appear in Chapter 4.

It is important that students recognize the need to work with *Challenger* regularly. This is often an issue for students in volunteer programs or institutions in which class attendance is not mandatory. Whatever the situation, if a student chooses to attend class on a highly infrequent basis, tell him politely but frankly that there is little point in his attending at all because he's not giving himself a chance to make any significant progress.

If only one class meeting a week is possible, try to schedule this class for 90 minutes to two hours. Also, have the students complete two lessons and, if appropriate, a writing activity for homework. When the students look at you as if you were crazy, show them that by completing a few components of the lessons each day, they will not only be able to do the work, but also reinforce what they are learning. Sports and music are helpful analogies because most students know that both require daily practice.

The Lesson Format

After the first class, which of course involves no homework review, the procedure for each lesson is basically the same. The overview below gives you an idea of what happens during each class. More detailed procedures for this work appear in later chapters of this manual.

1. **Writing assignment.** If students have been given a writing assignment, begin the class by letting them share their work in pairs or small groups. Chapter 5 gives details on writing assignments.

2. **Homework review.** Discuss the reading selection to make sure students have understood it and to give them a chance to react to the reading. Then go over the comprehension questions and the other exercises and have students make any necessary corrections.

3. **Reinforcement activity.** If no writing assignment was given and if time permits, have the students do one or more reinforcement activities. See Chapter 4 for suggestions about reinforcement activities.

4. **Homework preview.** Go over the Words for Study listed at the beginning of the lesson. Introduce the reading selection and call attention to any special features that may be new or confusing. Have students quickly preview the individual exercises for anything they don't understand.

Following this general procedure on a fairly consistent basis helps students because they tend to feel more relaxed and work better when they have a sense of routine. Modifications in the procedure should be made only when they will enhance students' reading development.

Just as you encourage students to see homework assignments as daily workouts, encourage them to see class time as a daily workout, also. These lessons should not be seen as achievement tests but rather as opportunities to move students smoothly toward their reading goals. Students do not have to demonstrate mastery of the material in one lesson in order to go on to the next lesson. Mastery will come with consistent practice.

It is crucial for teachers to think in terms of improvement rather than mastery because students using these books often want to add a fourth component to the lesson format—rationalizing and/or lamenting their mistakes. This uses up valuable classroom time and, if allowed a foothold, will result in students' giving up and dropping out. Students must learn to perceive their mistakes as a natural and helpful part of the learning process. They can learn this only by your gentle but firm reminder that consistent practice is the key to mastery.

Remember that both adult and adolescent reading students tend to be overly sensitive to mistakes in their work. In most cases, they firmly believe that if they hadn't made so many mistakes in the first place, they wouldn't have to be working in these books. For example, a woman in her mid-twenties who decided to quit class explained her reason this way: "My teacher told me that it was all right to make mistakes, but every time I had one in my work she would kind of close her eyes and shake her head like I should have learned all this in the fourth grade." Teachers must think and act in terms of improvement rather than mastery and regard mistakes as natural and helpful.

Do not expect to know at the outset how much time to allot to each segment of the lesson. Understanding exactly how to pace the lessons takes time. By paying attention to students' responses and rate of accuracy, you will gradually learn how to schedule the lessons so that students improve their reading and writing skills in a relaxed but efficient manner.

Preparing the Lessons

In preparing the lessons, develop the habit of following this procedure:

1. Familiarize yourself with the lesson students are to work on that day.
2. Review the appropriate lesson notes in Chapter 7 of this manual for suggestions to help you teach the lesson. Go over the appropriate answers in the Answer Key as well.
3. Review any notes you took after the preceding class in which you jotted down vocabulary words or writing difficulties that students need to review. Teacher note-taking is discussed in Chapter 6 of this manual.
4. Decide upon any reinforcement activities you may want to use and complete any preparation needed. Suggestions for reinforcement activities are given in Chapter 4.
5. Skim the lesson to be assigned for homework and the appropriate lesson notes so you can introduce the reading selection and answer any questions students may have about the exercises.

Last and most important, you need to prepare yourself mentally and emotionally for the class. If possible, take several minutes before the students' arrival to unwind from the previous activities of the day. As a general rule, how well the lesson goes is determined by how relaxed and focused you are on the work. As the teacher, your main function is to serve as a smooth bridge between the student and the lesson material. Your own patience and concentration will determine how helpful this "bridge" is.

The Teacher-Student Relationship

Making sure that you are relaxed for the lesson also contributes to the development of a good working relationship with your students. Adolescent or adult reading students rely heavily on your support and encouragement.

It is helpful to remember that most of us, as we grow older, learn to fake or avoid situations in which we feel inadequate. We prefer habits and routines that are familiar and give us some sense of security. Adolescent or adult reading students have entered into a situation in which they can neither avoid (unless they give up) nor fake their way through the material. They are to be admired for having put themselves in this situation. Unless they are extremely motivated or thick-skinned, they must feel a sense of support from you or they will eventually drop out, because exposing their lack of knowledge just gets too painful after a while.

In addition, completing the lessons in these books *is*

hard work. No matter how much progress is being made, virtually all students experience a sense of frustration at one time or another. Your encouragement will help them to get through these gloomy periods when they are ready to throw in the towel.

Suggestions for a Good Working Rapport

The following are suggestions to help you consider how best to develop a good working relationship with your students.

- Strive for naturalness in your voice and mannerisms. Some teachers unconsciously treat reading students as if they were mental invalids or victims of a ruthless society. A condescending or pitying approach does not help students become better readers.
- Greet the students pleasantly and spend a few minutes in casual conversation before you actually begin work. As a rule, do not allow this conversation to exceed five minutes. Students will take their cue from you. If you encourage conversing rather than working, they will be more than willing to oblige.
- Participate fully in this pre-lesson conversation and listen attentively to the students' remarks. Often you can later refer to these remarks when you are helping students to understand a vocabulary word or a point in the reading selection. Not only do they appreciate the fact that you actually were listening to them, but also they begin to make connections with the material they are studying.
- Use a phrase such as "Shall we get started?" to indicate that it is time to begin the lesson. A consistent use of such transitional statements helps the students feel more comfortable with both you and the class routine.
- If possible, work at an uncluttered table rather than at desks. Try to have straight-backed, cushioned chairs since physical comfort makes developing a good relationship easier.
- Be sure to use positive reinforcement during the lesson. Remind students of the progress they are making. When a student is particularly discouraged, do this in a concrete way. For example, show him how many pages of work he has completed, or have him look at his composition book to see all the writing he has done.
- Develop the habit of wishing students a good day or a good evening as they leave the class. This is especially important if both you and the students have had a rough session. The students, particularly adolescents, need to know that you don't carry personal grudges.

Classroom Supplies

For each class, students need to bring their *Challenger* book, their composition book, and a pen or pencil. The use of the composition book—a slim, loose-leaf binder with wide-lined paper—is discussed in Chapter 5.

You need your own copy of *Challenger*, any notes and reinforcement activities pertaining to the lesson, a few sheets of blank paper for notes, and a pen. A pen is recommended because students can spot your marginal notes and corrections more easily. Avoid red ink as it is frequently associated with too many bad memories.

Have a dictionary and, if possible, a set of encyclopedias, a globe or an atlas within easy reach. The encyclopedia and the dictionary are valuable resources because they provide pictures and additional information about many of the words, people, and events mentioned in the reading selections and exercises. Be prepared to teach students how to use these resources. Do not assume that students working at a Book 7 reading level are familiar with them.

A globe or map is helpful because it can make the facts presented in the lessons more meaningful to students. For example, in Lesson 2, Exercise 1 of Book 7, students are asked for the name of the town where the Pilgrims from the *Mayflower* landed. Many students don't know the location of Plymouth, Massachusetts. This presents a good opportunity to locate it on a map.

Encourage students to research additional information as often as their interest, abilities, and time permit and give them all the assistance you can when they need help. These mini-research experiences help students feel more competent when searching for information.

A Summary of Do's

1. Do try to schedule at least two classes each week which meet at a regularly-appointed time.
2. Do take time to develop a consistent lesson format that will work well for your students.
3. Do perceive your students' work in terms of improvement rather than mastery.
4. Do take time to prepare for each class.
5. Do give yourself a few moments to relax before each class.
6. Do develop a good working relationship with students because it is essential to their reading progress.
7. Do make sure that the environment in which you teach is as conducive to good learning as possible.
8. Do have reference and resource materials available, if possible.
9. Do give the students positive reinforcement during the lessons.

3. Teaching the Lessons

In this chapter, suggestions are given for teaching the main components of each lesson. These components include word study, the reading selection, the exercises, correcting the homework, and the homework preview.

Word Study

The *Challenger* series places a great deal of emphasis on learning and/or reviewing word meanings since a major obstacle to reading development is a poor vocabulary. It has been estimated that only about 2,000 words account for 99% of everything we say. To be a proficient reader, however, one must be familiar with far more than 2,000 words. Thus, except for the reading comprehension exercises, most of the other exercises focus on vocabulary development.

Word Charts and Definitions

As mentioned previously, the word charts contain new words that are organized around common phonics principles. Most of these principles have been introduced in earlier books and are being reviewed in Book 7. How much emphasis you give to the phonics principles depends upon the needs of your students. Some students enjoy reading the chart words aloud, while others prefer to start each class with the definitions exercise. Words from the chart are repeated frequently in Book 7 exercises, so it is not essential that students read the chart words aloud. For those who do, however, emphasize pronunciation only. Meanings are stressed in the definitions exercise and in many other exercises.

Words for Study

Keep in mind that the *Challenger* series is a controlled vocabulary series. When students wish to know how the words listed in the Words for Study at the beginning of each lesson have been selected, inform them that these words are appearing for the first time in the series. Most of the other words in each lesson have appeared earlier in the series.

Students not only find the concept of a controlled vocabulary interesting, but some interpret this concept in interesting ways. For example, one student who was experiencing difficulty with a synonym exercise in Book 6 remarked: "Well, you can't expect me to know words that were studied in Book 5!"

Behind this statement is a conviction shared by many reading students that once you've studied a word, you should never have to study it again. Unfortunately, this is not true. Words are learned through repetition, practice, and using the dictionary. Do not assume that your students know this. Simply remind them, when appropriate, that a good reading vocabulary is necessary for good reading and that they will encounter a word in various types of exercises so that they can truly master its meaning.

The best way to encourage your students as they complete the many vocabulary development exercises is to demonstrate an interest in language yourself. This does not mean that you have to use a lot of "fancy" words when talking to your students. What it does mean is that you do not approach vocabulary study as if it were something merely to be endured.

Suggestions for Enriching Word Study

Here are a few suggestions for making vocabulary study more interesting for students:

1. Have students pronounce the Words for Study in the next lesson during the homework preview. Most words will not give them any trouble. By pronouncing the unfamiliar ones, students will gain confidence in their ability to learn the word, and confidence often leads to interest.

2. Encourage students to develop the habit of paying attention to word endings. Words listed in the Words for Study appear in the same form in which they appear in the reading. For example, notice that in Lesson 1, *transacted* is listed. Emphasis on accurate pronunciations of endings will help students with both their reading and writing.

3. When time permits, spend a few minutes in casual conversation about some of the words. Using the Words for Study in Lesson 2 as an example, you may wish to talk about the two ways the word *liable* can be used, or have students identify the root in *penitentiary*, or help them trace the origin of *rheumatism* in a good dictionary. Occasional discussion of words helps students to see them as more than just a string of letters.

4. Take time during discussions of the readings to highlight vocabulary and/or language features. In Lesson 2, students enjoy substituting other colloquial expressions for some of the ones in the letters. These brief discussions help students to see that language patterns vary from group to group and that language is always changing.

5. Finally, strive to speak with expression. You needn't be a Broadway star, but a little ham goes a long way.

The Reading Selections

The amount of time you allot to oral reading and discussion of the reading selections ultimately depends on both the needs of your students and how much class time you have with them.

Oral Reading

Having students read aloud at least part of the reading selection periodically gives you an opportunity to note their strengths and weaknesses and also to help them develop good oral reading habits. Some students are under the impression that good oral reading means that one reads as fast as one can. Remind these students that in oral reading one must always be conscious of the needs of the listeners.

Discussing the Reading

Have a general discussion of the reading selection to refresh students' memories and to make sure they have understood the reading. Then discuss their responses to the comprehension exercises.

To create an atmosphere in which the reading selections and student thoughts about them can be discussed with a sense of harmony and unity, consider these suggestions.

1. Plan questions that you want to ask in class. Be prepared, however, to put your planned questions aside when a spontaneous question arises in class.

2. Make sure students understand the basic ground rule of all good discussions: one person speaks at a time.

3. Encourage participation, but don't force it. Likewise, discourage students from monopolizing the discussion.

4. Keep the discussion focused.

5. Avoid asking "yes" and "no" questions. Discussions, like travel, should be broadening. "Yes" and "no" questions shut off discussion by being answerable in a single word. They also imply that the student should have reached a conclusion before the discussion has even started.

6. If students seem confused by your questions, rephrase them rather than repeating them word-for-word. This practice is not only courteous, but it also reminds students that there is usually more than one way to phrase an idea.

These suggestions represent the easier part of moderating a discussion. The harder part is staying out of the way. Your task as the moderator is to get students to react to each other's opinions and comments, not to dominate the discussion yourself.

It is essential to view discussions in the same way that you view the students' other work—in terms of improvement, or growth, instead of mastery. It takes time to develop a good discussion group in which participants can learn to really listen to each other and gain confidence to express themselves as genuinely as possible. Do not expect it to be otherwise.

Through these discussions, students begin to sense a relationship between the lesson material and their own lives. The relationships they have with you and the other students can become more relaxed and real. This, in turn, means that everyone learns better and faster.

The Exercises

In the exercises, students develop their reasoning abilities because they are required to think and infer, to use context clues, to practice the process of elimination, and to apply what they already know to new situations.

Three points that you should emphasize to students are accuracy, legibility, and completeness. They are to spell their responses correctly and legibly, and they are not to leave any item blank. Tell them to answer all questions to the best of their ability. Not only does learning thrive on corrected mistakes, but also much is to be said for the art of intelligent guessing.

Remind students to check over their homework after they have finished all the exercises to make sure they have answered all questions completely and accurately.

Allow enough time at the end of the class period for previewing the exercises that are to be completed for homework. It is important that students understand exactly what is expected of them, so don't rush this segment of the lesson.

You should spend a few minutes during the first class meeting with your students to review the importance of homework. Remember, some of your students haven't been in a school situation for quite a while, and they may need to be reminded of the importance of completing the assignments as well as they can.

Sometimes students try to complete the homework right after a full day's (or full night's) work, or just before going to bed, or while they are trying to fulfill other responsibilities. Suggest that they schedule a definite, 30-minute study time in quiet surroundings when they are not exhausted.

Make sure to present your ideas on how to develop better study habits in the form of suggestions. You are not stating policy; you are simply encouraging students to think about how they can better achieve their reading goals within the circumstances of their lives.

Correcting the Homework

Be sure you allow enough time to go over the homework with the students. You will probably need to observe your students and try out a few different schedules before you hit on the pace that works best for them. But once you establish the appropriate pace, consistency promotes good concentration and effective learning.

Of all the lesson segments—the words for study, the reading selection, and the exercises—the exercises should be covered most thoroughly. All the homework should be corrected. Remember that many patterns are being established. If students develop the habit of doing something incorrectly, they will have a hard time unlearning the procedure. Be sure to explain this to the students. Eventually, they adapt to this procedure because they see that the more they correct in the early stages, the less they have to correct later.

Too often, going over the homework can be nothing more than a dry, mechanical routine in which students simply read their answers. Not only does this deprive them of practice with the words and concepts they've been studying, but also it is unfair. Consciously or unconsciously, the students' efforts are being slighted if the homework critique is being done in a dreary, "what's-the-answer-to-number-2?" style.

Take your time and enjoy this part of the lesson. If opportunities arise for brief tangents in which items are related to life experiences or other bits of information, take advantage of them.

Above all, don't forget to express your appreciation for students' efforts. Your supportive remarks should be brief and spoken in a natural voice. Excessive praise is ultimately as counterproductive as no praise at all. Words of encouragement should stress the notion of progress because students are progressing as they complete each lesson.

The Homework Preview

During the homework preview the students note what to do in the next lesson, which they are to complete for homework. Begin by going over the words listed in the Words for Study. Then introduce the reading selection to give students an idea of what they will be reading about. It may be necessary to help students get into the habit of noting the title of the reading selection. They should understand that the title gives them a general idea of what the selection is about and helps to focus their attention.

Remind students to refer to the reading selection when they cannot recall an answer to a comprehension question. In many instances, they may need to make intelligent guesses based on information which is implied rather than stated directly.

At this point in their reading development, all students are able to skim through the exercises and ask questions about words and/or directions with no assistance from you. The individual lesson notes indicate those instances in which you may want to emphasize certain words or directions.

A Summary of Do's

1. Do take time when necessary to explain to students how vocabulary study, the reading selections, and exercises contribute to their reading development.

2. Do make vocabulary study as interesting as possible.

3. Do encourage students to have an attitude of growth rather than fixed opinions in their discussions.

4. Do remind students, when necessary, of the significant role that homework plays in reading development.

5. Do emphasize the need for thoroughness, correct spelling, and accuracy in completing each exercise.

6. Do strive for completeness and enthusiasm in the homework reviews.

7. Do support the students' progress by taking the time to point out growth they have demonstrated in their work.

8. Do allow enough time at the end of each lesson to go over the Words for Study, introduce the next reading selection, and preview the homework exercises.

4. Reinforcement Activities

As the term suggests, these activities are designed to reinforce the students' understanding and retention of the lesson material. All students and most teachers occasionally need a break in the routine. Reinforcement activities may throw your schedule off a bit, but it's worth it. Just make sure that you leave enough time at the end of the class period to preview the homework.

At this point in students' development, two types of activities are particularly helpful:

- Activities which reinforce vocabulary skills.
- Occasional, short exercises which focus on mechanical or usage errors most of your students repeatedly make in their compositions.

The types of activities you use and the frequency with which you use them depend on the needs of your students and how often you have an opportunity to meet with them. The suggestions in this section are based on activities that students have found both helpful and enjoyable. This list is by no means complete. Take some time to develop your own "bag of tricks." Through talking with other teachers, skimming puzzle magazines, and using your own imagination, you will soon have reinforcement activities for a variety of skills. Students, too, often recall helpful activities from their earlier schooling. In fact, some of the suggestions which follow come from students.

Word and Information Games

Students working at this level often enjoy games that are modeled after television shows such as *Jeopardy*. These activities take some time to prepare, but they are an excellent way to reinforce vocabulary and information presented in the lessons. Certainly you can prepare the questions, but having the students do it gives them an excellent opportunity to review the material.

Students can create their own *Jeopardy* games by preparing sets of questions based on the reading selections. They can also create sets of vocabulary questions. For example, all the answers in a category might begin with the prefix *pre-* or the letter *s*. Other appropriate categories include: State Capitals, Bodies of Water, U.S. Presidents, Roman Gods and Goddesses, Famous Inventors, Abbreviations, and so on.

Other game show formats can also be used. For example, students enjoy playing their own version of *Wheel of Fortune*. They also enjoy their version of *College Bowl* in which two teams compete against each other. In this game, the teacher can prepare the questions and act as the moderator.

Puzzles

Many puzzles and other activities can be found in puzzle magazines sold in most drugstores and supermarkets. You can create your own puzzles using these formats and vocabulary from past and current word indexes. The word indexes for Book 7 are at the back of this manual. If you have access to a computer, there is software available for creating crossword puzzles into which you can insert vocabulary words to be reinforced.

Spelling Bees or Drills

This activity is most helpful when a specific principle is emphasized; for example, selecting words which all contain a specific suffix or consonant blend, or which belong to the same word family. Again, the word indexes at the back of this manual can be helpful in developing these activities. Drills should be spontaneous, brief—10 words is usually sufficient—and informally presented. In other words, they should not resemble a quiz in which students demonstrate mastery. Rather they are an opportunity to help students to better understand certain language principles that are giving them difficulty.

Worksheets

One type of worksheet can focus on some principle that is giving students trouble, such as recognizing analogies, using context clues, or making inferences. A popular type of worksheet for context clue or vocabulary reinforcement is to collect sentences from a newspaper or magazine in which troublesome words you have been working with appear. Set them up in a fill-in-the-blank format for the students to complete as a group. As one student once remarked, "You mean people actually do use these words?" You might also tell students to be on the lookout for these words and have them bring to class examples that they find in their own reading.

Another type of worksheet can give students practice with some aspect of writing, such as capitalization or punctuation. For example, many students neglect to use commas after introductory clauses. You might prepare ten sentences which begin with introductory clauses and have the students insert commas appropriately. Students find this type of introduction to grammar both tolerable and beneficial because it helps them to recall a rule they need for their own writing.

Enrichment Projects

Students can spend some time in the library seeking additional information about people or topics presented in the lessons and informally report their findings to the class. These reports can be given during the time set aside for reinforcement activities.

Any additional information that you can present also heightens the students' interest in the material. For example, for Lesson 6, some pictures of the Nazi army marching and of concentration camp survivors can help students to understand this period in world history a little better. Other enrichment ideas are suggested in the individual lesson notes.

Activities Based on Student Needs

Occasionally students may have specific personal needs, such as filling out an application form or creating a resume, that can be fit comfortably into the lesson format as reinforcement activities if they tell you about them far enough in advance. However, reinforcement activities are to reinforce, not replace, the lessons. If students are spending most of their valuable class time hearing additional information about the reading selections or getting your assistance with personal needs, they may learn some interesting facts or get forms filled out, but they are not progressing in their reading development.

If you suspect that students are using reinforcement activities to avoid working on the lessons, you probably need to help them clarify their learning goals. Gently but firmly remind them that, in the long run, their reading and writing will progress more rapidly if they concentrate more on the lesson work and recognize that the primary reason for reinforcement activities is to do just that—reinforce.

A Note to the Teacher

Because it takes time to prepare many of these reinforcement activities, be sure to file them away for use with future students.

Also, do not pressure yourself to come up with something new every time you plan a reinforcement activity. It takes a few years to develop a solid file of activities.

A Summary of Do's and Don'ts

1. Do make sure the scheduled lesson time is not sacrificed for reinforcement activities.

2. Do involve the students in planning and creating reinforcement activities whenever possible.

3. Do plan and implement activities that address both the students' learning needs and their personal needs.

4. Do remember to save materials you develop for future use.

5. Don't foster a "here's-some-more-hard-work" attitude toward reinforcement activities. The students have just finished discussing a reading selection, reviewing their homework, and learning new material. If the reinforcement activities are to benefit them, they need a little more informality from you for this segment of the lesson.

6. Don't foster a "this-is-just-for-fun" attitude either. Students might not find the activities enjoyable. And you want students who do find them enjoyable to recognize that pleasure and learning can go hand in hand.

5. Writing

Because the major purpose of this reading series is to help students develop their reading skills, less emphasis has been placed on writing skills. Even though writing is an important skill, it is a distinct skill that requires a great deal of practice and instruction time. Generally, the writing activities included in Book 7 focus on clarity and completeness of expression, coherence of thought, basic grammar, and spelling. However, there are plentiful opportunities for students to express their own opinions and ideas in writing.

Why Writing Is Included

The teacher can assume that a student who has completed some of the books which precede Book 7 can write complete sentences and coherent paragraphs. These students will not be surprised at the exercises which involve writing in the later *Challenger* books.

Students who are new to this series may wonder why writing activities have been included in a reading series. When this is the case, take time to point out the following:

* Writing is part of literacy. To be literate, a person must be able to write as well as read.

* Writing helps students to formulate and express their thoughts more precisely. This type of thinking helps them to complete the other exercises more rapidly.

* The writing that students do in these lessons will help them with other types of writing they may want to do, such as letters, reports, and short paragraphs on job applications or resumes.

* Only through actually writing can students see that they are able to write.

Opportunities for Writing

In Book 7, primary emphasis is placed on content, rather than on the mechanics of writing. The reading comprehension questions require students to draw conclusions from inferences, to cite reasons to support their opinions, to give explanations for their answers, and to cite examples and details to support their responses. There are also opportunities for imaginative writing, such as predicting the endings to stories and writing dialogues.

The individual lesson notes include many suggestions for writing assignments which can supplement the lessons as reinforcement activities. As stated in Chapter 1, it is recommended that weekly writing assignments of 250-500 words be given. However, the decision on how often to give writing assignments as homework should depend on the teacher's assessment of the students' time, personal needs, and capabilities. The key word is flexibility.

How to Handle Writing Assignments

When students have been given a writing assignment, have them share their work at the beginning of the next class session. Working in pairs or small groups, students can read their assignments aloud to one another and react to each other's writing on the basis of content and organization. Students can then exchange papers and act as editors or proofreaders, checking for mechanical problems such as missing words, spelling, capitalization, and punctuation. Give students the opportunity to revise their assignments before collecting them at the following class session.

When responding to these writing assignments, try to make positive comments as well as noting areas for improvement. Your reactions should be based more on the content, style, and organization of the writing than on the mechanical aspects.

It is recommended that students keep all writing assignments in a slim, loose-leaf binder with wide-lined notebook paper. Composition books enable both the students and the teacher to quickly review student progress. Have them date their work. As the weeks and months progress, most students enjoy looking back now and then at all the writing they have done and how much they have accomplished.

Like reading and vocabulary work, writing must be seen in terms of improvement rather than mastery. Most students read far better than they write. It is not uncommon for a student working in Book 6, for example, to write at a Book 4 level: very simple sentences, few modifiers, and underdeveloped thoughts. The most common reason for this is lack of practice. Allow students to develop from their own starting points, making them aware of their strengths as well as helping them to work on their weaknesses. And don't forget to be patient.

Here are a few suggestions to consider in helping students with their writing:

* As often as possible, have students read their written responses or compositions aloud. Students usually enjoy doing this, and it gives them a chance to hear whether or not their writing makes sense. Insist on honest but courteously presented reactions from the other students.

* Occasionally, allot some class time to studying how the professional writers write. Use a reading selection from *Challenger* or an interesting magazine article. Help students analyze the piece of writing on the basis of content organization and style. Make sure students understand that the writing they are analyzing is more than a second, third, or fourth draft. Few students recognize the contribution editing makes in the writing

process, and understanding this makes them feel less discouraged about their writing difficulties.

● With their permission, use writing from previous or present students as models to explain a particularly difficult writing assignment. Seeing the work of their peers often helps students realize that the teacher is not asking them to do the impossible.

● With their permission, compile a worksheet using sentences from student work which illustrate common mistakes. For example, a worksheet comprised of student-created run-on sentences is an excellent reinforcement activity. Students can work together in class to correct the errors and better understand how to avoid this particular writing problem.

● Provide the opportunity for students to publicly display their final drafts so other students can read them.

Dealing with Typical Writing Problems
Run-on Sentences

This situation demands consummate tact on your part because, invariably, the student thinks he has written a terrific sentence and is dismayed to learn that he has to divide it into three or four shorter sentences. Help him to see that, by using commas and periods wherever necessary, he helps readers to follow his thoughts more easily. To illustrate how punctuation helps the reader, have him read the sentence aloud, telling him to pause only at commas and to take a breath only at a period. If you prefer, you can demonstrate by reading his sentence to him. When he recognizes the value of punctuation marks, have him revise the run-on sentence as necessary. Be sure to commend him for his effort in helping to make his writing easier for readers to comprehend.

Omitted Words

When reading their sentences aloud, students are often surprised to see that they have omitted words. Remind them that many writers have this problem because the mind can think faster than the hand can write. Suggest that after they have written something, they should read it to themselves, pointing to each word as they encounter it. This strategy will help them learn to monitor their writing.

Confusing Sentences

When a student writes a sentence which is confusing, tell him you don't understand what he's trying to express and ask him to explain what he meant. Once you understand his intent, start a more coherent version of his sentence and have him finish it. After the student has read the revision, ask him if it matches what he meant. If not, work on the sentence until the revision accurately expresses the student's original idea.

Problems with Content and Organization

Students often have difficulty finding enough to say in their writing assignments and organizing their thoughts in a logical or interesting manner. Suggest that they begin by making notes of everything they can think of pertaining to the topic. The next step is to select from their notes the specific points and details that they want to include in their composition. Then they should organize those points and details in the order in which they want to include them. They should do all of this *before* writing their first draft. After the first draft is written, they should read it to see if they want to add anything more or to rearrange any of the points.

A Summary of Do's and Don'ts

1. Do tailor writing assignments to meet the students' needs and capabilities.
2. Do make sure that students understand the purpose and value of writing practice.
3. Do have students keep an orderly composition book for all their writing.
4. Do make sure that written work is evaluated, and when appropriate, have students write at least a second draft.
5. Do provide opportunities for students to share their writing with each other.
6. Don't expect the students' writing levels to be as high as their reading levels.
7. Don't allow writing assignments to become more important than the lessons and other necessary reinforcement activities.

6. Using the Lesson Notes

Because you are already familiar with the principles and procedures that pertain to the lessons in general from reading the previous chapters in this manual, you have the necessary foundation for sound instructional practices. The lesson notes address some specific points for the individual lessons. As part of class preparation, you should review the notes for the lesson assigned for homework. You should also read the notes for the lesson which you will be previewing to decide on how best to introduce the reading and to note any suggestions and reminders that might be helpful to the students when they are doing their homework.

Keep in mind that the lesson notes are only suggestions based on the experience of other reading teachers. If you try one of the suggestions a few times and find it doesn't work, disregard it.

Items of Primary and Secondary Emphasis

In most cases, the items listed under the "Primary emphasis" heading deal with comprehension of literature and vocabulary development. Using context clues and writing complete sentences often receive primary emphasis, also. The first time a particular task is introduced as an exercise, it also is listed under "Primary emphasis."

Items listed under "Secondary emphasis" receive less emphasis in the lesson. Many are skills which have been introduced previously and are now being reinforced. Occasionally, an item normally receiving secondary emphasis, such as analogies, is listed under "Primary emphasis" because more emphasis than usual has been given to a particular skill in order to review and assess the students' progress.

The Reading Selection

The lesson notes contain suggestions for introducing the reading selections and for discussing them. The reading segment of the lesson demands more flexibility on the teacher's part than any other. Students vary greatly in ability and motivation. Remember that the key to helping students make the greatest gains in the least amount of time is observation. Carefully monitoring your students' progress will help you to develop sound procedures for improving reading and comprehension skills.

Developing Your Own Notes

Develop the habit of keeping your own notes. Take time at the end of each class session to write down any remarks or reminders about particular difficulties students may have had with the lesson. Also make note of specific words or skills for which you may want to develop reinforcement activities.

Be sure to also keep notes of any procedures and techniques which seem to work well. Often you will hit upon an excellent way to present a certain skill or concept. Take some time to jot down your idea, especially if you know that you won't have the opportunity to use it again until a much later time. So much patience and concentration is called for in teaching reading that it's easy to forget those great ideas.

7. Lesson Notes for Book 7

Lesson 1

Review of Long and Short Vowels

Primary emphasis
- Comprehension of literature (short story)
- Vocabulary development (definitions)
- Writing complete sentences
- Using context clues

Secondary emphasis
- Predicting characters' responses
- Relating fictional events to personal experience
- Vocabulary review (Which Word Does Not Fit?)
- Review of long and short vowels

Word Chart

The Word Chart presents a systematic form through which students are introduced to new words in this reading series. Although it is not necessary to stress phonics principles, occasional reminders are helpful. For example, many students pronounce *eke* "eck." By pointing out that the silent *e* at the end indicates that the first *e* is long and jotting down a few other examples in which this rule applies, students are reminded of a principle that they can apply to other unfamiliar words.

A good rule of thumb for all the word charts in Book 7 is to avoid mentioning phonics rules unless an explanation would be clearly helpful. Since the main purpose of the word chart is to introduce words that have not appeared previously in the *Challenger* series, intensive phonics work is neither necessary nor productive at this point in the student's reading development.

Although students usually enjoy reading the words aloud, it is not imperative that they do so. Some students especially enjoy reading the word chart as a warm-up activity; others prefer starting each class with the definitions and replacing any word chart time with oral reading.

Do not dwell on the definitions when reading chart words. Students will encounter troublesome words in the exercises.

Exercise 1: Definitions

For these exercises, students should use both the process of elimination and a dictionary. Students can and should be expected to complete these exercises with 100% accuracy. If a student consistently makes two or more mistakes on definitions exercises, spend some time helping him to pinpoint the reasons for his errors. Always encourage students to learn from their mistakes rather than to see them as signs of failure.

A major reason that students complain about having to learn definitions is that they do not understand the significance of vocabulary work. Make sure students understand that knowing the meanings of words is vital to reading comprehension.

In all exercises in which copying is involved, students should copy accurately. There should be no spelling mistakes. All misspelled words should be corrected. This pattern (cruel as it seems) is more helpful than daily or weekly spelling tests in helping students to establish good spelling habits. When this expectation of accuracy is gently but consistently encouraged, the students themselves will begin to adopt a standard of accuracy and demonstrate more patience and pride in the quality of their work.

Story

The Words for Study section contains words that appear in this lesson for the first time in this controlled-vocabulary reading series.

Tell students that the reading selections which appear in this book are adapted from well-known, critically-acclaimed works. It motivates students to know that they are reading widely-respected material rather than, as one student expressed it, "stuff for problem students."

Review the terms *fiction* and *nonfiction*. Adolescents in particular often ask, "Is this really true?" Do not expect students—adolescents or adults—to automatically be able to distinguish between fiction and nonfiction.

Introduce the story by drawing students' attention to the title and asking what a stockbroker does. You may want to mention that O. Henry is famous for his surprise endings.

Generally, initial readings should be done for homework, but because this is the first lesson, allot time for an oral first reading in class. Begin by reading the first part of the story yourself, and then ask for volunteers to continue.

After reading the story aloud, discuss it in a general way. This gives students a chance to get a sense of the story as a whole while giving you the opportunity to assess their comprehension skills.

When you have completed the general discussion of the story, preview the exercises to be done for homework. Since this is the first lesson, take plenty of time and be sure all students understand how to do each exercise. If necessary, have students complete an item in each exercise during the preview so that they have a thorough understanding of how to do the work. Discuss the importance of homework. As suggested earlier, you might compare it to the daily practice that sports and music require.

Exercise 2: Understanding the Story

During the homework preview, remind students that they are to refer to the story when necessary, rather than to guess or to leave an answer blank. Students are to complete *all* the questions for all exercises. Some students seem to think that having to refer to the story for an answer is a sign of poor reading. Tell them that, on the contrary, it means they are good students!

Make sure all students are familiar with the process of elimination, which will help them complete many of the exercises in this book.

Exercise 3: What Do You Think?

When going over the answers during the homework review, make sure that students have used complete sentences. Initially, students may have difficulty putting their answers in sentence form, but with practice they will become increasingly proficient. Also, make sure that their answers reflect an understanding of the story. For example, suppose that in answer to question 1 a student writes that Harvey Maxwell would have said "Get lost!" Remind the student that Harvey had just gotten married, and help him to see that there is nothing in the story to indicate that Harvey would react in such a gruff manner.

Exercise 4: Which Word Does Not Fit?

During the homework preview, tell students to use the process of elimination and, if necessary, a dictionary to complete this exercise.

Exercise 5: More about the Stock Market

During the homework preview, tell students to read each entire sentence before attempting to find the correct answer. Tell them to pay attention to word endings and context clues in deciding which word to place in each blank. Also, they should not feel they must complete the sentences in the order in which they appear. If necessary, remind them that checking off words after they have used them is a helpful practice.

When students have finished filling in the blanks, have them read the entire passage again for comprehension.

During the homework review, discuss how suffixes provide important clues in identifying the correct answer.

Note

After students have gone over the exercises and made any necessary corrections during the homework review, give them an opportunity to ask questions or to make comments about what they have just accomplished. If they seem overwhelmed, point out strengths they have shown in completing the work. Remind them that this is only the first lesson and that they will get used to the work more quickly than they think possible.

Lesson 2
Review of Consonant Blends: Part 1
Primary emphasis
- Comprehension of literature (short story)
- Vocabulary development (definitions)
- Writing complete sentences
- Writing brief paragraphs
- Using context clues
- Using standard English

Secondary emphasis
- Idiomatic expressions
- Using the dictionary
- Review of consonant blends

Word Chart and Definitions

Use the procedure suggested for Lesson 1. Some students are not familiar with the *Mayflower* in definition 6. If time permits, bring in some additional information and a picture.

Story

During the preview, introduce the story by pointing out that it is a series of letters between a husband and wife.

Students may need to read this story more than once before comprehending all the subtleties. A good many inferences must be made in order to understand the plot and answer the comprehension questions. In the general discussion during the homework review, point out some of the facts which are presented in subtle ways, such as the fact that Ernie is a blackmailer.

Exercise 2: Understanding the Story

If students were unable to answer the questions correctly, you may need to review the process of using clues which the author provides to draw conclusions. Discuss "reading between the lines."

A suggested follow-up writing activity is to write a letter to a relative. Students often enjoy writing a letter in the style of Judy's first letter to Walt, describing all the terrible ordeals they're confronted with which make it impossible to keep up with personal correspondence.

Exercise 3: What Do You Think?

The students' opinions about Walt's mental abilities should reflect an understanding of the story. For question 2, some students may argue that Walt, not God, did most of the "providing." This offers a good opportunity to discuss the concept of irony.

Exercise 4: Standard English

During the homework preview, discuss how most people speak a variety of dialects. Discuss the fact that some of these dialects are more formal than others. People often use an informal dialect when they are talking with their family and friends. This informal way of speaking is perfectly acceptable in informal situations. But when people are talking in a more formal situation—to strangers, to supervisors at work, in school, at public meetings, and so on—it is often to their advantage to use a more formal dialect, standard English. Give students the opportunity to discuss their feelings on this issue. If appropriate, also mention that standard English usage is included on the GED Test.

Preview the exercise by discussing the meanings of each pair of words. Tell students to refer to these definitions when completing the exercise. Review the definitions during the homework review.

Exercise 5: Common Expressions

If necessary, remind students to use the process of elimination and to check off words as they use them. Also, students need not feel that they must complete the sentences in order.

Some of these expressions may be unfamiliar to students. This can give rise to a discussion of idiomatic expressions in general. Encourage students who are interested in the origins of any of these expressions to do a mini-research project. There are many popular works on etymology available.

Exercise 6: Look It Up

This exercise is a good opportunity to remind students that many words have several quite different and unrelated definitions.

Lesson 3

Review of Consonant Blends: Part 2
Primary emphasis
- Comprehension of literature (short story)
- Vocabulary development
  1. Definitions
  2. Synonyms
- Writing a brief paragraph
- Using standard English

Secondary emphasis
- Reasoning and spelling (Can You Crack the Code?)
- Review of consonant blends

Word Chart and Definitions

For number 1, you may want to point out during the homework review that although *credentials* is a plural word, its definition is singular.

Story

During the preview, note that this story is in two parts. Students will be reading only the first part for this lesson. During the review, have students speculate on how they think the plot will develop and what the conclusion will be.

Exercise 2: Understanding the Story

When students are doing exercises, encourage them to look up the meanings of any unfamiliar words.

Exercise 3: What Do You Think?

A follow-up discussion topic that students have found interesting is the opposite side of the question: Does performing good deeds usually lead to performing more good deeds?

Exercise 4: Synonyms

Remind those students who get tired of using the dictionary "all the time" that words are reviewed frequently in this book and learning them becomes easier with practice.

Exercise 5: Standard English

As in Lesson 2, go over each pair of words and the examples during the homework preview. Go over them again during the review. After the students have made any necessary corrections, spend a few moments reviewing the material discussed in Lesson 2.

Exercise 6: Can You Crack the Code?

Although these puzzles require quite a bit of work, students generally enjoy them. If necessary, help them get off to a good start by having them put *S's* above the *V's* and *P's* above the *A's*. Once they understand the procedure for cracking the code, they have little difficulty completing this exercise correctly.

Lesson 4

Review of Consonant Blends and Digraphs: Part 3
Primary emphasis
- Comprehension of literature (short story)
- Vocabulary development
  1. Definitions
  2. Antonyms
- Writing complete sentences
- Using context clues

Secondary emphasis
- Putting events in sequence
- Writing a brief paragraph
- The suffix *-al*
- Using references to locate factual information
- Review of consonant blends and digraphs

Word Chart and Definitions

Students often find many of the words on this particular chart difficult to pronounce. You may wish to review the pronunciation of the more troublesome words, such as *strychnine*.

Story

Introduce the story by reviewing what happened in Part I and remind students of some of their speculations about how the story will end. In the general discussion during the review, help students to understand the story as a whole by reviewing both parts. Discuss how close students came in their predictions.

Exercise 2: Understanding the Story

With the exception of the first one, which is done for the students, all of the events in question 1 happen in the second part of the story. During the homework review, have students read the sentences aloud in the order in which they took place.

Exercise 3: What Do You Think?

Students enjoy discussing or writing about their own opinion of this old saying.

Exercise 4: Words That End in *-al*

During the preview, remind students to read the entire sentence before attempting to fill in the blank with the correct answer. Review the term *suffix*.

Exercise 6: Look It Up

Students who have small, abridged dictionaries will probably need an encyclopedia to complete this exercise.

Review: Lessons 1-4

As in the earlier books in the *Challenger* series, it should be emphasized to the students that this is a review, not a test. Material is often presented in new ways to both challenge the students and arouse their interest. Preview each exercise included in the review as you do in the other lessons. An overall score of 80% or better on the review should be considered excellent.

Exercise 1: Word Review

Students may need to be told that the dates in parentheses in definitions 3 and 13 are the years in which the person was born and died.

Exercise 2: Synonyms and Antonyms

A suggestion that many students find helpful for this exercise is to complete all the synonyms before tackling the antonyms.

Exercise 3: Word Families

A helpful suggestion for this exercise is to encourage the students to read the sentences aloud so they can hear how the words sound in the sentences.

Exercise 4: Which Word Does Not Fit?

Number 8 usually gives students difficulty. During the preview, suggest that students use a map for this one. If students wonder if looking up the location of a state or country on a map is cheating, remind them that this is not a test.

Exercise 5: Money

Students should be encouraged to use a dictionary to complete this exercise. They should be discouraged from guessing. Some students miss number 11 because they don't realize that a missing apostrophe constitutes a misspelled word. Remind them of this.

Exercise 6: A Final Note on Love and Money

During the preview, read the poem aloud to the students. Allow them an opportunity to read it aloud during the homework review. To help those who have difficulty reading poetry, have students take turns reading sentences. This practice helps students break the habit of thinking that a line of poetry is always a complete sentence.

Since many students enjoy elaborating on the theme of love versus money, question 5 makes a good follow-up discussion topic.

You may wish to assign a composition to bring this unit of work to a conclusion. Here are some suggestions for composition topics relating to the theme of love and money:

1. Which Is More Important—Love or Money?
2. Love Is More Important to Me Than Money Is
3. Money Is More Important to Me Than Love Is
4. What I Would Do for Love
5. What I Wouldn't Do for Money

Lesson 5
Review of Digraphs: Part 4
Primary emphasis

- Comprehension of literature (short story)
- Vocabulary development (definitions)
- Writing complete sentences
- Identifying characters' feelings and reactions
- Analogies
- Using standard English

Secondary emphasis
- Predicting a character's response
- Relating the story to personal experience
- Classifying information (the *ch* sound)
- Review of consonant blends

Word Chart and Definitions

Have the students locate Chile on a world map or globe. Many students are surprised to see how "skinny" it is. Whenever a country or city is mentioned in a lesson, it is a good practice to have the students locate it on the map.

Story

To introduce this story, you may want to discuss briefly parent-child relationships and the things children do which disappoint their parents. As a follow-up writing topic, students might describe an experience which led them to see someone in a new light.

Exercise 2: Understanding the Story

Because this comprehension exercise is quite different from previous comprehension exercises, it may be a good idea to preview it more carefully than usual. Discuss the meanings of any unfamiliar words and have the students either give examples or use the words in sentences. A brief discussion about changes in feelings and reactions is also helpful.

Exercise 3: What Do You Think?

Students often enjoy elaborating on their responses to question 1.

Exercise 4: Word Relationships

Students often have difficulty with this type of exercise. When necessary, help students get started by completing the first question during the preview. Ask them to explain the relationship between *shepherd* and *flock*. Then have them read the four choices and decide which pair of words expresses a similar relationship. Most students will see that a *cowboy* tends a *herd* as a *shepherd* tends a *flock*.

Some students have trouble answering multiple choice questions. Encourage them to first eliminate the obviously incorrect answers. Then have them evaluate the remaining choices to select the correct ones.

Exercise 5: Sounds for *ch*

Students either complete this type of exercise with no effort at all or have a great deal of difficulty matching the words with the correct sounds. Encourage those who have difficulty to complete the exercise aloud so they can hear the sounds.

Exercise 6: Standard English

As before, preview each set of words and go over the examples. During the homework review, the material from Lessons 2 and 3 should be reviewed, also.

Lesson 6
Review of Consonant Blends: Part 5
Primary emphasis
- Comprehension of literature (short story)
- Vocabulary development
  1. Definitions
  2. Synonyms and Antonyms
- Writing complete sentences

Secondary emphasis
- Relating fictional events to personal experience
- Comparing characters from different stories
- Spelling
- Using references to locate factual information
- Review of consonant blends

Story

Students often are unaware of the prejudice with which Jews have been confronted historically and the role of this prejudice during World War II. Any additional materials, particularly pictures, which present a more comprehensive portrait of these times can be helpful. Remind those students who worked in the earlier books in this series of the excerpts from *The Diary of Anne Frank* in Lessons 12 and 13 of Book 4.

In the general discussion during the review, help students to see the parallels between the events in the story and the events which actually occurred during the war.

The concept *point of view* provides the basis for a good follow-up discussion. Have students consider how the story might have developed had it been narrated by the father, a policeman, or any other character.

Exercise 3: What Do You Think?

Both questions 1 and 2 are good topics for further discussion. In discussing question 2, remind students that Halper wrote this story in 1938, before the start of World War II. Since he couldn't have known the extent of the persecution that the Jews of Europe were to suffer, his story was certainly prophetic.

Exercise 5: March, 1938

Two of the incorrect words in this exercise are spelled correctly. Because of the context, however, the following are incorrect:
  1. Sentence 3—*then* should be *than*
  2. Sentence 11—*passed* should be *past*
Some students may also miss number 10 because they forget that a missing apostrophe constitutes a misspelled word.

As a follow-up activity, you might have students consider how facts, opinions, and ads in today's newspapers are different from the way they appeared in 1938. Copies of newspapers from years ago can stimulate a lively discussion.

As a reinforcement activity you might have students copy sentences from a current newspaper in which they underline five words and intentionally misspell one. You can then duplicate them and you have a student-made spelling test.

Exercise 6: Who Was General Pershing?

Again, if time permits, bring in pictures and/or interesting articles pertaining to World War I to give students more of a sense of this period of history.

Lesson 7
Review of Consonant Blends: Part 6
Primary emphasis
- Comprehension of literature (short story)
- Vocabulary development (definitions)
- Writing complete sentences
- Using standard English

Secondary emphasis
- Classifying
- Using references
- Chronological order
- Review of consonant blends

Word Chart

There are several unusual words in this chart, such as *squiggle, tweak, twerp*, and *twiddle*, which you may wish to draw to students' attention.

Story

To avoid giving away the point of this story too soon, introduce it by discussing the tensions involved in taking a driver's test. Students may want to briefly share their experiences in this situation.

Exercise 3: What Do You Think?

For number 2, if students notice the 1940 copyright date, instruct them to find clues in the story that indicate that it was written a number of years ago.

A discussion about the nature of prejudice can be launched by comparing and contrasting the prejudice in "The Test" with that in "Prelude." Some questions that may be considered are: How does prejudice create tension? How do bystanders often respond? How do prejudiced people show their hostility?

Exercise 5: Chronological Order

If students don't have access to an almanac, a good dictionary or an encyclopedia will contain the necessary information in separate entries. During the preview, discuss how to go about finding this information. You may

wish to have the students record additional information also. For example, for the American presidents, they could write the term of office after each president's name. For the holidays, they could write the date.

Exercise 6: Standard English

Preview the material as before. During the review, go over the material covered in Lessons 2, 3, and 5. If students are having difficulty with this material, consider creating a worksheet with sentences based on the examples in all four of these lessons as a reinforcement activity.

Lesson 8
Review of Vowel Combinations: Part 1
Primary emphasis
- Comprehension of literature (short story)
- Vocabulary development
  1. Definitions
  2. Matching things with tasks
  3. Puzzle (Find the Quote)
- Writing complete sentences
- Using context clues

Secondary emphasis
- The suffix *-ly*
- Spelling (changing the *y* to *i*)
- Review of vowel combinations

Story

To avoid giving away the surprise ending, introduce the story by briefly discussing "first days" in general. Parents might recall their feelings on sending their children to school for the first time. Or students might discuss their feelings on the first day of a new job or in a new class. During the review, ask students when they first suspected that Laurie and Charles were one and the same.

Exercise 2: Understanding the Story

Students—particularly adults—find it helpful to discuss ways in which adults protect themselves from pressure by inventing or imagining things. A suggested composition topic is "The Charles in Me."

Exercise 3: What Might You Use if You Wanted To...

Students may not be familiar with some of these words, such as *compost, grid, spectacles*, and *sauna*. Remind them to use their dictionaries for unfamiliar words.

Exercise 6: Find the Quote

If students are encountering this type of puzzle for the first time, have them complete a few of the items during the homework preview. Have them fill in the appropriate blanks in the quotation as they answer each of the items. In this way, they can work back and forth between the clues and the quotation, using context clues in the quotation to complete the partially filled-in words.

During the review, students enjoy swapping tricks they developed to help them solve the puzzle. They also enjoy hearing any tricks you might have developed for problem-solving.

Review: Lessons 1-8

Remind students that this is a review, not a test. These exercises give additional opportunities to review words and concepts that were introduced in previous lessons. Encourage them to refer to those lessons or a dictionary for definitions they cannot recall. An overall score of 80% or better on review exercises should be considered excellent.

Exercise 3: Sound Review

Encourage students to complete this exercise aloud so that they can hear the word in which the sound is different.

Exercise 4: Word Families

Remind students that it is also helpful to read these sentences aloud to hear which word fits best in each blank.

Exercise 5: Standard English: A Review

During the preview, remind students to check the material in Lessons 2, 3, 5, and 7 when doing this review exercise.

Exercise 6: A Poet's Thoughts

During the preview, read the poem aloud to the students. Give them the opportunity to read the poem aloud during the homework review. Spend some time relating the theme of "Uphill" to a few of the characters in this set of short stories.

If you wish to assign a composition to conclude this unit of work, here are some suggestions for composition topics relating to the theme of struggle:

1. Putting up with Parents
2. Being a Single Parent
3. How Prejudice Holds Me Back in Life
4. Why I Am Prejudiced
5. How Fantasy Helps Me Get Through the Day
6. Life Is a Constant Struggle

Lesson 9
Review of Vowel Combinations: Part 2
Primary emphasis
- Comprehension of literature (myth)
- Vocabulary development (definitions)
- Using context clues
- Using standard English

Secondary emphasis
- Analogies
- Using references to locate information
- Review of vowel combinations

Words for Study

Spend a few moments discussing these words during the homework preview. For many students, this will be their first exposure to a myth, and an understanding of the words will help to make this a more enjoyable reading experience for them.

Story

During the preview, discuss the term *myth*. Students who have worked in previous books in this series are familiar with several mythological characters, including Cupid, Apollo, and Midas. Be sure they understand who Odysseus was and what a Cyclops was. Mention Odysseus's Roman name, Ulysses, which may be more familiar to students. In the general discussion during the review, you may want to relate some of the other adventures Odysseus and his men had before finally returning home.

Exercise 3: More about Odysseus

During the preview, remind students to read the entire passage after they have filled in the blanks.

The two number choices in this exercise provide a good opportunity to remind students of the value of context clues and of reading ahead before deciding where each word goes.

Students may be interested in reading more episodes from *The Odyssey*. Excellent translations of this work in which the language is simplified can be found in most libraries. As a follow-up writing activity, students enjoy creating their own "myths" complete with gods and goddesses and adventurous escapades.

Exercise 4: Word Relationships

Although students are familiar with this exercise format, they may have difficulty with one or two of the questions. In question 4, the meaning of *fast* is "to go without food," and *recruit* in question 6 is a noun, not a verb.

Exercise 5: More about Standard Usage

Preview each set of words and the examples, as before. If time permits, review the material in previous lessons as well.

Exercise 6: Gods and Goddesses

The Roman names for these gods may be more familiar to students than the Greek ones are, since all but Minerva are also the names of planets. Remind them of Odysseus's Roman name, Ulysses.

Lesson 10

Review of *r*-Controlled Vowels
Primary emphasis
- Comprehension of literature (short story)
- Vocabulary development (definitions)
- Using context clues

Secondary emphasis
- Writing complete sentences
- Predicting characters' responses
- Vocabulary review (puzzle)
- Review of *r*-controlled vowels

Words for Study

Many students are intrigued with the words *Buddhist* and *purgatory* and wish to know more. Help them locate additional information. Students who are willing to give a brief report to their classmates should be encouraged to do so.

Story

To introduce this story, you may want to talk briefly about Pearl S. Buck, a popular writer who grew up and worked in China and wrote several books about China and the Far East. Point out that this story, like the one in Lessons 3 and 4, is in two parts. Inform students about the Japanese invasion of China in 1937, prior to the outbreak of World War II. Be sure students know where China and Japan are located. Pictures of Chinese villages and people help students to visualize the setting, also.

Exercise 3: What Do You Think?

Discuss students' responses to question 2 and encourage them to predict how the story will end. The title should give students a clue. A follow-up discussion can be based on the question: Do you think that there are people anywhere in the world today who don't know what airplanes are?

Exercise 4: China

As a follow-up, interested students may want to select a specific topic about China, such as the language, traditional clothing, Buddhism, etc., for a mini-research project. They could report their findings orally or in writing.

Exercise 5: Spelling Check

Students not familiar with this type of puzzle may need to complete an answer or two during the homework preview. Remind students to check off the syllables as they use them. They need not work in the order in which the clues appear. If students recognize the country and capital from the map, they can fill in the names and then they will have the initial letters of each of the answer words. Make sure students capitalize the answers to numbers 7, 11, 12, and 16.

Lesson 11

Review of *r*-Controlled Vowel Combinations
Primary emphasis
- Comprehension of literature (short story)
- Vocabulary development
  1. Definitions
  2. Words that describe and don't describe
- Using context clues

Secondary emphasis
- Vocabulary review
- The suffix *-ness*
- Review of *r*-controlled vowel combinations

Story

During the preview, briefly review the story so far and the students' predictions of how Mrs. Wang will react as the story progresses. In the general discussion during the review, help the students to understand the story as a whole by reviewing both parts. Discuss how close they came in their predictions of Mrs. Wang's reactions. Make sure students know about the final outcome of Japan's war against China.

Two follow-up composition ideas for this story are "The Circumstances under Which I Would Be Willing to Sacrifice My Life" and "My Definition of Courage."

Exercise 3: Word Review

During the preview tell students that both words in a set must make sense in the sentence. They should use the process of elimination and context clues to select the correct set. Remind them to take their time and use dictionaries when necessary.

Exercise 5: Words That *Don't* Describe

Finding a negative match is a bit harder than the matching in Exercise 4. During the preview, be sure students understand how to complete this exercise.

Lesson 12

Vowels Followed by the Letters *w* and *l*

Primary emphasis

- Comprehension of literature (short story)
- Vocabulary development (definitions)
- Writing complete sentences
- Proverbs
- Using standard English

Secondary emphasis

- Word families
- Using context clues
- Review of vowels followed by *w* and *l*

Story

To introduce this story, you might point to similarities with "The Old Demon," such as the fact that an attack is imminent and a family is in danger. Avoid any mention of the setting. In the general discussion during the review, make sure students understand what happened in the story.

Students usually benefit from a discussion about the issue of nuclear weapons. Encourage them to explore issues related to this subject that concern them. You might launch a discussion by asking how students think the children in the shelter will get along.

Exercise 3: What Do You Think?

These questions can lead to a general discussion of the importance of selection of detail and order of presentation in storytelling.

Exercise 4: Proverbs

This exercise is particularly difficult for students who are unfamiliar with these proverbs. Encourage these students to get help from those who are familiar with some of the proverbs. During the homework preview, a brief discussion about the value and durability of proverbs is recommended. During the review, discuss the meanings of any proverbs the students don't understand.

Any of these proverbs provides an excellent topic for a composition in which the students explore the truth of a proverb in terms of an experience they have had.

Exercise 5: More about Standard English

This is the last material about standard English formally introduced in this book. Preview it as before. Allot time during the review to go over the material studied in Lessons 2, 3, 5, 7, and 9. If students continue to have difficulty with some of this material, appropriate reinforcement activities should be used.

Some students are interested in learning more about the atomic bomb. Excerpts from John Hersey's book *Hiroshima* are recommended as a helpful follow-up activity.

Review: Lessons 1-12

As before, remind students that this review is not a test but an additional opportunity to practice words and concepts introduced in previous lessons. An overall score of 80% should be considered excellent.

Exercise 2: Which Word Does Not Fit?

In number 1, some students may argue that Old Maid is the correct answer because it is a children's game. However, Old Maid can be played by adults, while solitaire must be played alone.

Exercise 4: What Is Often Said When...

Some of these expressions may not be familiar to all students, and a dictionary may not be much help. Suggest that they use the process of elimination or seek the help of a friend. During the review, discuss any expressions that students do not understand.

Exercise 5: A Review of Standard Usage

Remind students to review the usage material they studied in Lessons 2, 3, 5, 7, 9, and 12 in completing this exercise.

Exercise 6: On Fear and Courage

Read the two poems aloud during the homework preview. Students will probably not have difficulty understanding the two poems so much as they will have trouble remembering relevant details about the characters in this set of stories. Remind them to skim the stories for details they may have forgotten. During the review, have the students read the poems aloud and share their answers to the questions.

If you wish to assign a composition to conclude this unit of work, here are some suggestions relating to the topic of courage:

1. The Most Courageous Event I Have Ever Witnessed
2. What I Fear the Most
3. My Most Courageous Moment
4. The Time Courage Failed Me
5. The Bravest Person I Know
6. How I Overcame My Worst Fear

Lesson 13

The Hard and Soft *g*

Primary emphasis

- Comprehension of literature (drama)
- Vocabulary development
  1. Definitions
  2. Synonyms and antonyms
- Writing complete sentences
- Writing brief paragraphs
- Understanding tone of voice
- Using context clues

Secondary emphasis

- Using references to locate factual information
- Review of the hard and soft *g*

Play

In introducing the scene, point out the characters' names and note the stage directions in italics. Explain that while these words are not spoken aloud, they should be read, because they give clues to the action of the play and to the characters' feelings. Explain also that this scene takes place near the end of the play. Ask if students have seen the very popular movie version of this play starring Henry Fonda and Katharine Hepburn. During the homework review, have students read the play aloud.

Exercise 2: Understanding the Play

In discussing these questions, help students to see that in reading a play, the meanings are communicated primarily through dialogue, unlike short stories, which have descriptive passages as well.

Exercise 3: What Do You Think?

Allow students to share their answers during the review. A follow-up discussion topic might be based on students' personal brushes with death.

Exercise 5: Tone of Voice

This exercise is good for oral reading practice because students can practice tone of voice. Have them take turns reading innocently, mysteriously, and so on.

Exercise 6: Vacations around the World

Have students locate at least some of these places on a map or globe. If time permits, have them list the words according to city, state, or country (exclude the two seas). Some students have difficulty distinguishing among these three divisions, and this type of exercise is helpful.

Follow-up composition topics for this exercise are "My Dream Vacation," "The Place I Would Most Like to Visit," and "My Favorite Trip."

Lesson 14

The Hard and Soft *c*

Primary emphasis

- Comprehension of literature (biography)
- Vocabulary development
  1. Definitions
  2. Identifying words that do not fit
  3. Matching people with things they know about

Secondary emphasis

- The suffix *-ist*
- Using references to locate factual information
- Puzzle (anagrams)
- Review of the hard and soft *c*

Words for Study

This set of words tends to be particularly difficult for students and should definitely be previewed in order that the reading can be better understood and appreciated.

Reading

During the homework preview, mention that this selection is taken from a biography about the famous Russian novelist, Fyodor Dostoyevsky. Be sure students understand what a *biography* is. Mention one or two of Dostoyevsky's best-known works, such as *Crime and Punishment* and *The Brothers Karamazov*. During the review, it is helpful to discuss tzars and their role prior to the Russian Revolution and the significance of the Russian Revolution in general. Any pictures of this period in Russian history are also very helpful.

Exercise 2: Understanding the Reading

After reviewing the comprehension questions, discuss in detail Dostoyevsky's reactions throughout this ordeal. You may want to contrast his brush with death with that of Norman in "On Golden Pond."

Exercise 5: Look It Up

If students are interested in learning more about Russia or Russian history, encourage them to select a topic for a mini-research project.

Exercise 6: The Mystery Tzar

If students are not familiar with this type of puzzle, have them complete a few of the items during the homework preview. Tell them to skip around, to skim, and to use the sums as clues. For example, most students immediately know that the answer for clue 7 is *angel*. If they skim the puzzle, they will usually spot *angle* without any trouble. Have them write *angel* on the line and put 7 in the circle. Remind them to write *a* on the blank numbered 7 at the bottom. If they fill in these blanks as they go along, they may guess the answer before the puzzle is finished. This, in turn, will give them the initial letters of the remaining words. Also point out that the clue numbers always add up to 34, both horizontally and vertically. This may help students to find the right answers and also to know whether or not they have the right answers.

Lesson 15

The Letter *y*

Primary emphasis
- Comprehension of literature (short story)
- Vocabulary development
  1. Definitions
  2. Words with multiple meanings
- Using context clues

Secondary emphasis
- Writing complete sentences
- Analogies
- Using a dictionary to locate factual information
- Homonyms
- Review of the letter *y*

Story

In introducing this story, mention that Hemingway is a very well-known author. Students may be familiar with some of his writings, particularly since movies were based on several of his works. In the general discussion, you may want to draw students' attention to Hemingway's straightforward style.

Since Hemingway is known for his terse dialogues, you might have the students write a dialogue as a follow-up activity. The dialogue can be written in the form of a script, and students can refer to Lesson 13 for a script format.

Exercise 2: Understanding the Story

During the homework preview, tell students that they will probably need to refer to the dictionary to answer questions 1 and 3. These questions are asking about the boiling point of water. You may want to mention that other substances boil at different temperatures.

Exercise 4: Multiple Meanings

During the preview, review the fact that a word can have more than one meaning.

Exercise 5: Working with Measurements

Answers to question 1 will vary slightly depending on how students arrive at the answer. Accept any figure that is approximately 80½ miles. Again, questions 4 and 5 refer to the freezing point of water.

Exercise 6: Homonyms

Homonyms are often a source of spelling difficulty for students. You may wish to follow up this exercise with a spelling quiz in which you say a homonym, use it in a sentence, and have the students write the correct spelling. This exercise is more effective if students discuss each correct answer immediately after writing it.

Lesson 16

The Sound for *ph*

Primary emphasis
- Comprehension of literature (short story)
- Vocabulary development (definitions)
- Contrasting characters' reactions
- Using context clues

Secondary emphasis
- Writing complete sentences
- Hyphenated words
- Review of *ph* sound

Story

To introduce this story, you might compare and contrast it with "A Day's Wait," mentioning that a central character is ill in both stories, but while Schatz only believed that he was dying, in this story the character really does face death. Point out that O. Henry also wrote the story in Lesson 1.

In addition to discussing the story as a whole during the review, you may want to discuss contrasts between O. Henry's writing style and that of Hemingway.

Exercise 3: What Do You Think?

Questions 2 and 3 in this exercise call for the students to contrast the reactions of characters from two different stories. For many students, this is not an easy activity. For this reason, the questions say, "Describe the difference..." rather than using the term *contrast*.

If you sense students are going to have difficulty with the concept of *contrast*, spend a few moments during the homework preview discussing this. Many students, for example, have found it easier to think about the difference between characters' reactions if they discuss briefly the difference between how they usually feel on a Monday morning and on a Friday afternoon. During this discussion, it is helpful if students also perceive how people often respond differently to the same situation. (Not all students hate Monday mornings!) By having a clear idea of what is expected of them for questions 2 and 3, students are more apt to take their time in sorting out the differences between Schatz's and Johnsy's reactions.

Exercise 4: Hyphenated Words

Make sure students do not forget the hyphens. Some students do not recognize that including hyphens in their answers is part of accurate spelling.

Exercise 6: The $24 Swindle

Remind students to read the entire passage through after filling in the blanks.

Some pictures of Greenwich Village or other parts of Manhattan in the 18th, 19th, and 20th centuries help students to visualize the changes which have taken place since the first Dutch settlement.

Review: Lessons 1-16

As with other reviews, remind students that this is not a test but an additional opportunity to practice words and concepts introduced previously. Encourage them to look back to previous lessons if necessary. An overall score of 80% should be considered excellent.

Exercise 4: Find the Homonym

During the preview, go over the example and make sure students understand what is expected of them. Point out that the numbered definitions are for the homonyms they fill in, rather than for the ones which appear on the page. They do not have to do these in order.

Exercise 5: A Poet's View of Dying

During the preview, read the poem aloud and explain that this is an excerpt from a longer poem. Have the students read it aloud during the review. Allot plenty of time to discuss the poem and their responses to the questions.

To conclude this unit of work about brushes with death, you may wish to consider one or more of the following:

1. A writing assignment in which students discuss their feelings about death.
2. A writing assignment in which students relate an experience in which they felt close to death and the meaning this experience had for them.
3. A writing assignment in which the student writes his own obituary, using examples from newspapers as models. This may sound morbid, but some students have found that this activity has helped them to focus on what they truly wish to accomplish in life.
4. A discussion in which the reactions of the characters in this unit are compared and contrasted.
5. A discussion about abortion or euthanasia. For this activity it is helpful to have students bring in newspaper clippings that pertain to these subjects. As in any valuable discussion, the emphasis should be on exploring and clarifying perceptions rather than clinging to one's own point of view.

Lesson 17
Silent Letters
Primary emphasis
- Comprehension of literature (folktales)
- Vocabulary development
  1. Definitions
  2. Matching adjectives with folktale characters
- Writing complete sentences
- Writing a paragraph

Secondary emphasis
- Comparing characters in different stories
- Using context clues
- Classifying
- Sequencing
- Review of silent letters

Folktales

Introduce the readings by discussing some of the qualities of folktales that make them different from short stories. Mention that folktales are generally anonymous, traditional tales that have been circulated orally before being written down, and that they are usually not set in a specific time or place. These folktales are particularly good for oral reading practice.

As a writing activity topic, students enjoy speculating on what they would do if they were given three wishes or the Gift of Luck. As a follow-up activity, you may wish to bring in more folktales for the students to read. *World Folktales* published by Charles Scribner's Sons is an excellent resource for this activity.

Exercise 2: Understanding the Folktales

The quotation in the "What do you think?" portion of this exercise can be used to launch a discussion of the students' own missed opportunities.

Exercise 3: Character Descriptions

As a follow-up writing activity, have students write a brief folktale in which they use some of the characters listed in the second column. For example, one student began his folktale: "Once upon a time a pooped peasant met a lowly woodcutter who lived at the edge of an enchanted forest."

Exercise 5: More about Armenia

Remind students to read the entire passage through after filling in the blanks.

Exercise 6: More about Black Pudding

Black pudding is also called blood pudding or blood sausage. Some students may be familiar with these names.

Lesson 18

Double Consonants

Primary emphasis
- Reading comprehension (nonfiction)
- Vocabulary development (definitions)
- Using context clues

Secondary emphasis
- Writing complete sentences
- Analogies
- Spelling (puzzle: state search)
- Review of double consonants

Reading

The concepts discussed by Erich Fromm in this selection are difficult for some students to grasp. In introducing the reading, help students to understand the contrast between *having* and *being* by pointing out that what a person *has* is not the same as what a person *is*. During the general discussion, be sure that students understand what Fromm means by "modes of existence." Have students summarize this selection as a group. Be sure they include all the major points.

Exercise 2: Understanding the Reading

Review the differences between the terms *story*, *autobiography*, *biography*, and *essay* during the homework review.

Exercise 3: What Do You Think?

Allow ample time to discuss students' responses to questions 2 and 3. A debate on these questions can help to further clarify the concepts Fromm discusses.

Exercise 4: Word Relationships

Although not specified in the directions, students should be instructed to write the answers out on the lines provided.

Exercise 5: On Latin and Language

During the preview, make sure students understand that they do not use all the words listed at the left. As a follow-up activity, students might look up the derivations of the Words for Study to see how many have Latin roots.

Exercise 6: State Search

If students are not familiar with this type of puzzle, point out the example and have them find one or two more states during the class period. When comparing answers during the review, you should note that while *Kansas* is listed separately, it is also contained in *Arkansas*. Either answer should be counted as correct.

Lesson 19

More Work with Two Consonants in the Middle of Words

Primary emphasis
- Comprehension of literature (drama)
- Vocabulary development
  1. Definitions
  2. Synonyms and Antonyms
- Using context clues

Secondary emphasis
- Writing complete sentences
- Word families
- Using the dictionary
- Classifying
- Review of two consonants in the middle of words

Play

To introduce this play, compare it with the scene from *On Golden Pond* in Lesson 13. While that was written for the stage, *The Woman Who Willed a Miracle* was written for television. Point out some of the differences, such as the use of a narrator and the very short scenes. Remind students that the stage directions give clues to the characters' actions and reactions and are not spoken aloud. Point out that this play is concluded in Lesson 20.

During the review, ask students to predict what will happen in the conclusion of the play. The title should give them some ideas. You may want to postpone an oral reading of the play until the review of Lesson 20, when it can be read from beginning to end.

A general discussion on the difficulties of living with a handicap may be appropriate. Students can share examples from their own experience or discuss famous people. A simple activity which helps students become more aware of how a handicap can make even easy things difficult is to have them blindfold themselves and then try to do a simple task, such as walk across the room, draw a simple picture, or write a sentence or two of dictation.

Exercise 5: Word Families

Unlike previous Word Families exercises, students select only one of the three word choices for each question.

Exercise 6: Using the Dictionary

A good dictionary is needed to complete this exercise correctly. If students have small, abridged dictionaries, you may decide to have them complete this exercise in class.

Lesson 20

Four-Letter Words

Primary emphasis

- Comprehension of literature (drama and poetry)
- Vocabulary development
  1. Definitions
  2. Finding the word that doesn't fit
  3. Matching people and problems

Secondary emphasis

- The prefixes *uni-*, *bi-*, and *tri-*
- Writing complete sentences
- Four-letter words

Play

Briefly review what took place in the first three scenes of the play, and remind students of their predictions about how it would end. During the homework review, have students read the play aloud. Discuss their predictions in relation to the outcome of the plot. Ask if they were surprised to find that the play was based on actual people.

A videocassette of this play is available at video stores or can be ordered directly by calling (800) 423-7455, extension 3425, and asking for Mailbox Video. In California, the number to call is (818) 888-3040. The cassette includes a brief documentary on the Lemke family produced by the Canadian Broadcasting Corporation. It offers an excellent follow-up activity for Lessons 19 and 20.

Exercise 5: A Little Latin

During the preview, make sure students understand how to do this exercise.

Exercise 6: On Living and Loving: A Poet's Point of View

As you did in previous lessons, read the poems aloud during the preview and have the students read them aloud during the homework review. During the general discussion of the poems and the questions, have students give reasons why the Lemkes would agree with Johnson's point of view.

As a follow-up writing activity, have students select one of the two poems and explain why they agree or disagree with the poet's point of view.

Review: Lessons 1-20

As with the other reviews, this last review is not to be perceived as a test, but rather as a final opportunity to work with many of the words and concepts introduced in Book 7.

Exercise 4: More Work with Expressions and Proverbs

During the homework review, discuss the meanings of any expressions or proverbs that are unfamiliar to the students.

Exercise 5: World Capitals

Have students locate the countries and their capitals on a map or globe.

Exercise 6: Find the Quote

Remind students to refer to Exercise 6 in Lesson 8 if they have forgotten how to do this type of puzzle.

After any necessary corrections have been made by the students during the homework review, spend some time reviewing and evaluating the students' progress. Compare the writing activities that they did in the early lessons with writing they have done recently. Many students, particularly those who began their work in the early books of the *Challenger* series, enjoy perusing the word index at the back of this manual, because it is a concrete representation of their accomplishment.

Answer Key for Book 7

Lesson 1

1 Definitions

1. hub	6. tot	11. ebb
2. option	7. imp	12. tote
3. maze	8. humdrum	13. eke
4. yen	9. impede	14. rove
5. zombie	10. kindle	15. puny

2 Understanding the Story

1. a	3. d	5. a	7. d
2. b	4. c	6. c	

3 What Do You Think?

1. Answers will vary. Reasonable responses include: He would be embarrassed that he had forgotten; he would be tender and apologetic to his new wife; he would bluff by saying he was only kidding.
2. Answers will vary. Accept any reasonable response.
3. Answers will vary.

4 Which Word Does Not Fit?

1. piano	5. fern	9. murmur
2. romp	6. crawl	10. messenger
3. creative	7. occurrence	
4. foam	8. thoughtless	

5 More about the Stock Market

agents, foreign, commission

ownership

stockholder, relays, partner, recorded, network

conditions, profit, loss

Lesson 2

1 Definitions

1. nucleus	6. Plymouth	11. plasma
2. glacier	7. blemish	12. Pluto
3. blazer	8. blunt	13. flog
4. clique	9. glee	
5. blunder	10. clergy	

2 Understanding the Story

1. He drove the getaway car for a bank robbery.
2. He says he didn't know the men planned to rob the bank or that they had guns. They paid him to get them out of town and that was all he did.
3. Ernie is a blackmailer.
4. a. Ernie has some letters that George, the vice president of the bank, wrote to Ruthie Watkins. When Judy mentions the letters to George, he arranges an extension on their mortgage payments for them.
   b. Knowing that his mail is read by prison authorities, Walt writes to Judy that something is buried in the south field. The sheriff and his deputies dig up the field looking for what they think will be the money from the bank robbery. Once the field is dug up, Judy can plant a crop.

3 What Do You Think?

1. Walt is not stupid. He figures out ways to get his mortgage extended and to get his field ready for planting while he is in prison.
2. Answers will vary. Accept any reasonable response.

4 Standard English

1. a. stupid	2. a. teaching	3. a. set
b. dumb	b. teach	b. sit
c. stupid	c. learn	c. sit
d. dumb	d. teach	d. set
e. stupid	e. learn	e. set

5 Common Expressions

1. goose, chicken	5. bug, tigers
2. flea, pig's	6. rat, horse
3. horse, hog	7. butterflies, bull
4. chicken, skunk	8. goat, dog

6 Look It Up

1. completely, totally, or any similar word
2. to measure the depth of something; to examine critically; to search
3. Answers will vary. Reasonable responses include: to hang a full-length mirror; to straighten a large picture frame.

Lesson 3

1 Definitions

1. credentials	6. privilege	11. fragrant
2. griddle	7. predicament	12. frequent
3. crocodile	8. drudgery	13. gruff
4. prude	9. drowsy	
5. drama	10. brilliant	

2 Understanding the Story

1. a	3. d	5. a	7. d
2. d	4. c	6. b	8. a

3 What Do You Think?

Answers will vary. Accept any reasonable response.

4 Synonyms

1. comical
2. glamour
3. inflict
4. mess
5. recently
6. acquire
7. unity
8. possibly
9. effortless
10. reflection
11. generous
12. flimsy

5 Standard English

1. a. may
   b. can
   c. May
   d. may, can
2. a. in
   b. into
   c. into
   d. in, into
3. a. borrow
   b. lending
   c. borrow
   d. borrowing, lending
4. a. about
   b. around
   c. about
   d. about, around

6 Can You Crack the Code?

1. spruce
2. oak
3. maple
4. birch
5. willow
6. pine
7. cinnamon
8. redwood
9. chestnut
10. Judas

Lesson 4

1 Definitions

1. shroud
2. throng
3. strychnine
4. Scrooge
5. sprockets
6. shrapnel
7. shrew
8. sprite
9. strife
10. shrewd
11. scrawny
12. threshold

2 Understanding the Story

1. 5, 4, 2, 6, 7, 9, 10, 1, 3, 8
2. In signing notes to buy the garage and later the auto dealership, Henry gambled that he would be able to pay off the notes without having to use the hidden money.
3. In the second part of the story, Henry's gambling is a legal and ordinary business risk which many people take. His gambling in the first part of the story was done with money that wasn't his, and was therefore illegal.
4. Answers will vary. Reasonable responses include: He was unwilling to destroy the spruce tree in order to get the stolen money. He returned $30,000 plus interest to the bank. His wife and children mattered more to him than the money did.

3 What Do You Think?

Robert Arthur seems to agree with the saying. When Henry cares more for his wife and children, and for the spruce tree, than he does for the money, he prospers and has a happy life. Jerome Smith, on the other hand, becomes involved in illegal activities in his pursuit of money and ends up in prison, as Henry did earlier.

4 Words That End in -al

1. brutal
2. intentional
3. disposal
4. refusal
5. proposal
6. approval
7. personal
8. regional
9. mechanical
10. behavioral

5 Antonyms

1. impede
2. flustered
3. creditor
4. glamorous
5. dwindling
6. shrinkage
7. rumor
8. ebb
9. idleness
10. detect
11. ordinary
12. approve
13. unity
14. precious

6 Look It Up

1. 75 mph
2. Atlantic
3. a lamp with a glass chimney covering a bulb, wick, or candle

Review: Lessons 1-4

1 Word Review

1. temple
2. suburb
3. Mozart
4. mortgage
5. compost
6. casino
7. plaza
8. burlap
9. gratitude
10. rheumatism
11. reptile
12. rumor
13. Dickens
14. parole
15. credit
16. finance

2 Synonyms and Antonyms

1. wicked, saintly
2. prolong, shorten
3. brilliant, drab
4. nucleus, edge
5. humble, boastful
6. trustworthy, faithless
7. glee, despair
8. frequent, seldom
9. rival, partner
10. humdrum, inspiring
11. puny, strong
12. anxious, calm

3 Word Families

1. finances, financially, financial
2. disunity, unify, unity
3. satisfied, satisfaction, satisfactory
4. fashionable, fashion, unfashionable
5. graciousness, graciously, gracious
6. shrewd, shrewdly, shrewdness
7. wicked, wickedly, wickedness
8. disagreeable, agreeably, agreeable
9. instance, instantly, instant
10. generous, generously, generosity

4 Which Word Does Not Fit?

1. plod	5. disagree	9. spree
2. grasp	6. amazing	10. earthquake
3. frustration	7. alter	11. option
4. angel	8. Illinois	12. outraged

5 Money

1. inches	5. budget	9. necessary
2. attempting	6. friend	10. usually
3. thankful	7. federal	11. don't
4. success	8. government	12. wealth

6 A Final Note on Love and Money

1. a. He offered her lands, houses, farms, pearls, rubies, laces, dresses, ribbons, and horses, i.e., riches, material things.
   b. He offered her a song, happiness, excitement, strength, gaiety, joy.
2. She chooses the second man.
3. Answers will vary. Reasonable responses include: She was attracted by the excitement, the happiness, the gaiety; she loved him; he made her happy.
4. Answers will vary. Some students may feel that the last line indicates that she regrets her choice. Other students may maintain that the playful tone of the poem indicates that this statement should not be taken seriously.
5. Answers will vary.

Lesson 5

1 Definitions

1. shawl	6. chandelier	11. chute
2. characteristic	7. orchid	12. shiftless
3. thoroughfare	8. Chile	13. chemistry
4. chauffeur	9. shanty	14. parched
5. merchant	10. theory	15. shun

2 Understanding the Story

Answers will vary. Reasonable responses include:

Sam Carr:
   puzzled: Mrs. Higgins wasn't reacting the way he expected her to.
   softhearted: Mrs. Higgins persuaded him not to call the police.

Alfred Higgins:
   blustering: He thought he could bluff his way out of the store.
   frightened: Sam Carr caught him with the stolen items in his pocket.
   astonished: His mother had been calm and dignified when he had expected her to make a scene.

Mrs. Higgins:
   polite: She was quiet and gentle in her manner with Mr. Carr.
   angry: Alfred had disgraced her again.

trembling: She had held her distress in check until she was alone.

3 What Do You Think?

1. Answers will vary. Accept any reasonable response.
2. Answers will vary.
3. Answers will vary.

4 Word Relationships

1. cowboy is to herd
2. Egypt is to Africa
3. strategy is to method
4. fixture is to chandelier
5. hymn is to church
6. Memphis is to Tennessee
7. thermometer is to temperature
8. oval is to shape
9. silliness is to gravity
10. bothersome is to convenient

5 Sounds for *ch*

china	chandelier	character
chalk	champagne	ache
chapel	chef	chemical
Cherokee	Chicago	choir
chief	machinery	echo
lynch	Michigan	mechanical
scorch	mustache	strychnine

6 Standard English

1. a. all ready	2. a. Besides	3. a. affect
b. already	b. beside	b. effect
c. already	c. Besides	c. effect
d. all ready	d. beside	d. affect

Lesson 6

1 Definitions

1. skirmish	6. smithereens	11. scan
2. slogan	7. microscope	12. descend
3. scholarship	8. telescope	13. scurry
4. descendant	9. slacken	
5. Scandinavia	10. snicker	

2 Understanding the Story

1. b	3. c	5. b	7. d	9. a
2. c	4. d	6. d	8. a	10. d

3 What Do You Think?

1. Answers will vary. Accept any reasonable response.
2. The bullying by the gang and the destruction of the newsstand were events which foretold the great violence against and persecution of Jews which was to come under Hitler's regime. The indifference of the people who witnessed the event and did nothing to stop it was also an

indication of the attitudes which made the genocide in Europe possible.

3. Answers will vary. Reasonable responses include: The Silversteins had done nothing wrong, while Alfred Higgins had caused his family's problems. The Silversteins' pressure comes from other people, and it is unfair and unjust, while the pressure on the Higgins family comes from within and is caused by their own actions and reactions.

4 Synonyms and Antonyms

1. antonyms	7. synonyms	13. antonyms
2. antonyms	8. synonyms	14. synonyms
3. synonyms	9. synonyms	15. synonyms
4. synonyms	10. antonyms	16. synonyms
5. antonyms	11. antonyms	
6. antonyms	12. synonyms	

5 March, 1938

1. schedule	5. priest	9. Wednesday
2. plainly	6. reference	10. You'll
3. than	7. beginning	11. past
4. jewelry	8. helpful	12. committee

In the city, a copy of the daily edition cost 3¢.

6 Who Was General Pershing?

1. John Joseph Pershing
2. September 13, 1860—July 15, 1948
3. the Spanish-American War and World War I (He also fought in several battles against the Indians in the West.)
4. 1914-1918
5. Black Jack

Lesson 7

1 Definitions

1. squadron	5. spatula	9. squatter
2. chromium	6. teamster	10. quest
3. squabble	7. chronological	11. whisk
4. swab	8. swine	12. tweak

2 Understanding the Story

1. Answers will vary. Alert students may notice the reference to "a white person" in the second paragraph and realize very quickly that prejudice is the theme.
2. Answers will vary. Reasonable responses include: Marian wants to earn her license because she deserves it. Marian knows that offering a bribe would only give the inspector another reason to reject her.
3. Answers will vary. Many students may cite the inspector's referring to Marian as "Mandy" as the first hint.
4. Any three details, including the following: He calls her "Mandy" and "Mandy-Lou." He says she is "old enough to have a flock of pickaninnies." He hints that she wants to

sneak out at night to meet "some young blood." He assumes she is from the South. He speaks to her in a phony Southern accent. He makes fun of her for having a college degree.
5. When Marian tells the inspector she got her college degree, her voice was "not quite steady."
6. Marian probably had little chance of passing, since the first inspector had marked mistakes she didn't remember and the second one deliberately goaded her into doing something wrong. He then marked four X's at random. He didn't judge her driving ability at all.
7. Mrs. Ericson doesn't seem to be aware that prejudice is a factor in Marian's inability to get a driver's license.
8. Answers will vary. Students may feel that if Mrs. Ericson had gone with Marian, the inspector wouldn't have goaded Marian into failing.
9. Answers will vary. Reasonable responses include: She fails to keep her self-control. She fails to act inferior, as she is expected to. She fails to hide her emotions. She fails to keep her cool.

3 What Do You Think?

1. Answers will vary. Students may suggest that Mrs. Ericson should stay with her, that they should go to a different town, that she should act the way she is expected to act, etc.
2. Answers will vary. Alert students will notice that the story was originally copyrighted in 1940.

4 Word Review

1. chandelier	6. Peru	11. strudel
2. Africa	7. husk	12. spleen
3. house	8. machinist	13. panther
4. flute	9. sun	14. banana
5. ivy	10. Dickens	15. sponge

5 Chronological Order

Presidents	Holidays
Thomas Jefferson	Good Friday
Andrew Jackson	Memorial Day
Abraham Lincoln	Fourth of July
James Garfield	Labor Day
Herbert Hoover	Columbus Day
John F. Kennedy	Veterans Day

6 Standard English

1. Change *no* to *any.*
2. Change *than* to *from.*
3. Change *no* to *any.*
4. Change *being that* to *since* or *because.*
5. Delete *here.*
6. Change *off of* to *off.*
7. Change *being that* to *since* or *because.*
8. Change *alright* to *all right.*

Lesson 8

1 Definitions

1. thyroid	6. peeve	11. loiter
2. cleaver	7. woe	12. heed
3. hoe-down	8. treacherous	13. queasy
4. foe	9. bloat	
5. moat	10. maim	

2 Understanding the Story

1. Any three of the following, or similar details: Laurie was rude to his father and mother. He swaggered and his voice became rough sounding. He used bad language. He spilled his sister's milk. He had to think before he gave Charles's name. He played the "Gee, you're dumb" joke on his father. He filled his wagon full of mud and pulled it through the kitchen.

2. Laurie's mother is curious about Charles's mother. She seems to pity her and wonder how Charles's mother could cope with such a child.

3. Answers will vary. She doesn't like Laurie's swaggering toughness and corrects his bad grammar. But she doesn't scold or punish him for his rudeness, and believes his bad behavior is a result of Charles's influence.

4. Laurie created Charles to be able to tell his parents about the things he did in school without having them punish or scold him for being so naughty. He could witness his parents' reactions to his behavior without being held accountable for his actions.

3 What Might You Use if You Wanted To...

1. explosives	6. compost	11. scraper
2. scissors	7. grid	12. spectacles
3. cleaver	8. burlap	13. slogan
4. stereo	9. telescope	14. sauna
5. microscope	10. plasma	15. griddle

4 The Suffix -ly

1. evident, evidently
2. responsibly, responsible
3. probable, probably
4. furiously, furious
5. spiritual, spiritually
6. indignant, indignantly
7. earnest, earnestly
8. physically, physical
9. casual, casually
10. smug, smugly

5 Spelling

1. shakily	5. thriftily	9. nastily
2. hungrily	6. sturdily	10. hastily
3. bossily	7. stockily	11. ordinarily
4. fancily	8. naughtily	12. extraordinarily

6 Find the Quote

1. footnote	6. itchy	11. New England
2. shoe	7. one-third	12. deflate
3. dynamite	8. scooter	13. timetable
4. telephone	9. litterbug	14. boulevard
5. bottle	10. dud	

Quote: I do not intend the children to be schooled, but to be allowed under the gentlest treatment to develop freely.

Review: Lessons 1-8

1 Word Review

1. lapse	6. stampede	11. pigment
2. prejudice	7. New Zealand	12. memorial
3. fragment	8. Iceland	13. scope
4. nursery	9. decree	14. dignity
5. schedule	10. republic	15. charity

2 Word Review

1. a	4. b	7. a	10. a	13. d
2. c	5. d	8. c	11. c	14. a
3. d	6. b	9. c	12. b	

3 Sound Review

1. senator	4. thyself	7. broadcast
2. plaid	5. science	8. laughter
3. discharge	6. chapter	

4 Word Families

1. apology, apologetic, apologize
2. disloyally, disloyalty, disloyal
3. incompetent, competent, competence
4. official, unofficial, officially
5. Unacquainted, acquaint, acquaintance
6. observer, observations, observed
7. residence, residential, resident
8. familiar, Familiarity, unfamiliar
9. respectful, respect, disrespect, respectable
10. determined, determine, determination, undetermined

5 Standard English: A Review

1. 2   2. 3   3. 1   4. 4   5. 5   6. 1

6 A Poet's Thoughts

1. Rossetti seems to consider pressures and problems common, as she speaks of the road winding uphill "all the way," the journey taking "the whole long day," and coming to the end "travel-sore and weak," seeking a resting-place.

2. Night represents the end of life.

3. The inn and the beds represent the shelter, comfort and rest of the afterlife in which Rossetti believed.

4. a. Answers will vary. Reasonable responses include: a young person looking for assurances; a disappointed, dejected or bereaved person.

   b. An older, wiser person who believes in the continuation of life after death.

Lesson 9

1 Definitions

1. grievance
2. typhoon
3. virtue
4. spouse
5. reign
6. revenue
7. residue
8. hygiene
9. siege
10. oust
11. vouch

2 Understanding the Story

1. a
2. c
3. a
4. c
5. d
6. b
7. d
8. c
9. b

3 More about Odysseus

hero, scholars, Homer, ninth
recounts, journeying, myth, probably, twelfth
Homer's, portrayed, shrewd, noble, however, character

4 Word Relationships

1. b
2. c
3. a
4. a
5. d
6. b
7. c
8. a
9. c
10. d

5 More about Standard Usage

1. a. altogether
   b. altogether
   c. all together
   d. all together, altogether
2. a. latest
   b. latest
   c. last
   d. latest, last
3. a. between
   b. among
   c. among
   d. between, among
4. a. preceded
   b. proceeded
   c. precedes
   d. preceded, proceeded

6 Gods and Goddesses

1. Neptune, god of the sea
2. Pluto, god of the underworld
3. Minerva, goddess of wisdom and the arts
4. Mercury, god of commerce and travel; messenger of the gods
5. Venus, goddess of love and beauty
6. Mars, god of war

Lesson 10

1 Definitions

1. hermit
2. proverb
3. narcotic
4. irksome
5. urban
6. rural
7. wary
8. threadbare
9. Saturn
10. Mercury
11. lurk
12. vary

2 Understanding the Story

1. b
2. c
3. c
4. a
5. d
6. a
7. c
8. d
9. b
10. d

3 What Do You Think?

1. Answers will vary. Reasonable responses include: If they had known about bombing, they would have evacuated the town more quickly. If they had known about bombs, they wouldn't have gone to see what had dropped from the sky.
2. Answers will vary. Accept any reasonable response.

4 China

1. vast, exceeded, populated, major, suitable, agriculture
2. previous, society, tradition, current, ordinary, official
3. former, ideal, units, formal, fair, legal
4. Chinese, China, foreigners, alphabet, characters, frequently
5. discouraged, traditional, standards, worshipped, appealed, strife

5 Spelling Check

1. knapsack
2. allowance
3. bamboo
4. undertaker
5. laundromat
6. apostrophe
7. February
8. garnet
9. hearsay
10. astronaut
11. Neptune
12. Ithaca
13. spearmint
14. tulip
15. amen
16. Newton

Capital: Kabul
Country: Afghanistan

Lesson 11

1 Definitions

1. boar
2. endearment
3. tourniquet
4. gourd
5. bleary
6. eerie
7. gourmet
8. lair
9. weary
10. yearn
11. impair
12. veer
13. peerless

2 Understanding the Story

1. a
2. a
3. c
4. c
5. b
6. b
7. b
8. d
9. d
10. a

3 Word Review

1. eerie — omen
2. wavering — resources
3. lion's — lair
4. irksome — courtship
5. Pearl Harbor — Hawaii
6. New York City — New York
7. Pilgrims — dull
8. courteously — bluntness
9. completed — betrayed
10. agreeable — frustrated
11. prude — displeased
12. instill — boldly

4 Words That Describe

1. severe
2. classified
3. treacherous
4. dismal
5. scarlet
6. romantic
7. feeble
8. steadfast
9. eerie
10. beige
11. hoarse
12. sincere

5 Words That *Don't* Describe

1. frizzy
2. unintentional
3. savage
4. apparent
5. heartfelt
6. persistent
7. hasty
8. generous
9. forgiving
10. nourishing
11. distinct
12. deafening

6 The Suffix *-ness*

1. suddenness, bluntness
2. drowsiness, feebleness
3. skimpiness, thriftiness
4. graciousness, queasiness
5. idleness, scornfulness
6. earnestness, casualness
7. scrawniness, sturdiness
8. cleanliness, godliness

Lesson 12

1 Definitions

1. kilt
2. scow
3. bolster
4. widower
5. brawl
6. culprit
7. stowaway
8. pulpit
9. widow
10. fowl
11. pew
12. jolt
13. jilt

2 Understanding the Story

1. Any three of the following or similar details: The husband and wife shared old jokes. The younger boy and girl played together. They all cooperated when the alert came. The father and oldest son worked closely together.
2. The mother thinks that the bomb shelter should be shared with others in an emergency. She feels that would be the religious thing to do.
3. He believes his responsibility is to save his own family, but no one else. He compares their situation to that of Noah and says that since the others were warned and didn't prepare, they were meant to die.
4. His wife gives up her place for someone else's child. He realizes that one or two more children could be saved if he gives up his place. Also, he doesn't want to go on without his wife.

3 What Do You Think?

1. Answers will vary. Accept any reasonable response.
2. The characters were probably not named so that the setting of the story would not be known, and also to underscore the idea that people living in different countries behave in similar ways.
3. The reader assumes that the story is set in the U.S. and therefore relates to the characters more closely. The point Neal makes is that people all over the world would act and feel essentially the same in the same situation.
4. Answers will vary. Accept any reasonable response.
5. Answers will vary. Accept any reasonable response.

4 Proverbs

1. d
2. a
3. b
4. c
5. a
6. c
7. b
8. d
9. d
10. c

5 More about Standard English

1. Change *because* to *that*.
2. Change *don't* to *doesn't*.
3. Change *might of* to *might have*.
4. Change *had ought* to *ought*.
5. Change *had ought* to *ought*.
6. Change *because* to *that*.
7. Delete *a* before *purple*.
8. Delete *a* before *prophet*.

6 Word Families

1. unrehearsed, rehearsed, rehearsal
2. achieved, unachieved, achievements
3. unnourishing, nourishing, nourishment
4. mournful, mournfully, mourning
5. unapparent, apparent, apparently
6. courteous, courteously, courtesy
7. sincerity, sincerely, sincere
8. suitable, unsuitable, suitable
9. persuasive, persuasion, persuade
10. misfortune, unfortunate, fortune, unfortunately

Review: Lessons 1-12

1 Word Review

1. volume
2. circuit
3. sluice
4. delicatessen
5. bristle
6. prairie
7. scoundrel
8. motive
9. odyssey
10. missile
11. retaliation
12. peso
13. verdict
14. atom
15. eternity
16. savage

2 Which Word Does Not Fit?

1. solitaire
2. jilt
3. withdrawn
4. Australia
5. endearment
6. qualified
7. unsafe
8. prairie
9. grieve
10. widower
11. shears
12. report
13. wield
14. advertise

3 A Review of Sounds

1. chemistry
2. tow
3. profile
4. gourd
5. bout
6. sleigh
7. weary
8. bargain
9. thorough
10. issue

4 What Is Often Said When...

1. a
2. d
3. b
4. a
5. d
6. a
7. a
8. d
9. b
10. a

5 A Review of Standard Usage

1. 2
2. 2
3. 1
4. 4
5. 3
6. 5

6 On Fear and Courage

1. Answers will vary. Reasonable responses include:
   (a) **What Odysseus fears:** Odysseus fears the giant Cyclops will kill him and all of his men.

   How he fights it: He outwits the Cyclops first by telling him his name is "Nobody," then by blinding him and tying his men and himself to the sheep so they can escape.

   (b) **What Mrs. Wang fears:** She fears that the Japanese will take their land.

   How she fights it: She opens the dike to drown the Japanese soldiers, even though she knows she will probably die doing it.

   (c) **What the wife fears:** She fears that her family and neighbors will die in a nuclear attack.

   How she fights it: She prepares for an attack, sees her children safely into the shelter, and then courageously gives up her place for another woman's child.

2. Answers will vary. Reasonable responses include:

   Odysseus: Although he was afraid they would all be killed, he didn't despair. He summoned his wits and tricked the Cyclops, freeing himself and his men.

   Mrs. Wang: She knew she was about to die, but she had lived a long, full life and believed that she might be able to get herself out of purgatory with her unselfish act.

   the wife: She knew that she would die, but she believed that saving a child's life was the religious thing to do.

3. Answers will vary. Accept any reasonable response.

Lesson 13

1 Definitions

1. gelatin	7. spigot	13. bigot
2. agenda	8. tragedy	14. vogue
3. generator	9. fungus	15. gangrene
4. hostage	10. outrageous	16. haggle
5. legend	11. fatigue	
6. logic	12. genuine	

2 Understanding the Play

1. He lifted and carried the heavy box full of china.
2. Most of their relatives and dearest friends have died.
3. They put Norman's book back on the shelf to be read next summer.
4. Answers will vary.

3 What Do You Think?

Answers will vary.

4 Synonyms and Antonyms

1. swarthy, fair	7. aimless, deliberate
2. eternal, temporary	8. outrageous, sensible
3. carefree, worried	9. withdrawn, outgoing
4. descendant, ancestor	10. courteous, crude
5. counterfeit, genuine	11. callous, warmhearted
6. zesty, tasteless	12. fatigued, energetic

5 Tone of Voice

1. innocently	5. grimly	9. wisely
2. mysteriously	6. persistently	10. absent-mindedly
3. coaxingly	7. formally	
4. encouragingly	8. grudgingly	

6 Vacations around the World

1. Boston	6. Washington, D.C.	11. Austria
2. Las Vegas	7. Jamestown	12. Greece
3. Philadelphia	8. Black Sea	13. Dead Sea
4. Atlantic City	9. Ireland	14. Hawaii
5. Amsterdam	10. Utah	15. Bethlehem

Lesson 14

1 Definitions

1. zinc	7. disciple	13. majestic
2. jaundice	8. columnist	14. mimic
3. cavity	9. Sicily	15. larceny
4 fabric	10. civilian	16. malice
5. tonic	11. citrus	
6. vacuum	12. menace	

2 Understanding the Reading

1. c	3. c	5. a	7. d	9. c
2. b	4. d	6. c	8. a	10. b

3 Which Word Does Not Fit?

1. Odysseus	7. enfold	13. alter
2. whimper	8. coconut	14. plague
3. cannibal	9. folly	15. distinct
4. courteously	10. Switzerland	16. vast
5. sphere	11. cultivate	
6. propose	12. bog	

4 Who Might Know Most About...?

1. receptionist	6. humorist	11. psychiatrist
2. pianist	7. tourist	12. naturalist
3. columnist	8. physicist	13. pharmacist
4. artist	9. motorist	14. chemist
5. colonist	10. typist	15. nutritionist

Question: -*ist* means a person who does something.

5 Look It Up

1. tsar, czar
2. An emperor or king, particularly one of the former rulers of Russia
3. 1868-1918
4. 1894
5. 1894-1917
6. He abdicated the throne in 1917 and was executed by revolutionary forces in 1918.

6 The Mystery Tzar

CRATE 16 TRACE	ASIDE 2 IDEAS	THERE 11 ETHER	CANOE 5 OCEAN
BLEAT 9 TABLE	ANGLE 7 ANGEL	STALE 6 LEAST	LEAFS 12 FLEAS
WEEPS 8 SWEEP	SHORE 10 HORSE	CAROB 3 COBRA	SLIDE 13 IDLES
TONES 1 NOTES	CAUSE 15 SAUCE	FLIER 14 RIFLE	SHORN 4 HORNS

The Mystery Tzar: Nicholas the First

Lesson 15

1 Definitions

1. synagogue
2. hydrogen
3. Syria
4. sentry
5. syringe
6. hypocrite
7. cypress
8. ebony
9. cynical
10. Sydney
11. foyer
12. analyze
13. waylay

2 Understanding the Story

1. 212° F
2. the doctor and the father
3. 100° C
4. Schatz
5. Schatz is waiting to die.
6. Schatz knows his temperature is 102° and he believes that people can't live with a temperature above 44°.
7. Answers will vary. Reasonable responses include: Schatz wasn't responding to his company. He thought Schatz might relax and sleep if he were left alone. The father may have wanted some fresh air and exercise. He knew Schatz wasn't seriously ill.
8. He tells his father that he believes he is going to die because his temperature is 102°. His father explains the difference between the Fahrenheit and Centigrade thermometers and convinces him that he isn't going to die.
9. Answers will vary. Accept any of the following or similar details: He didn't sleep nor move. He stared at the foot of the bed. He wasn't interested in the story his father read to him. He wouldn't let any others come into his room.

3 Word Relationships

1. cider is to pudding
2. nightstick is to patrolman
3. prowler is to lurk
4. fragment is to piece
5. advise is to listen
6. clove is to garlic
7. Denver is to Colorado
8. traditional is to customary
9. waggle is to waddle
10. nutty is to cuckoo

4 Multiple Meanings

1. b   2. d   3. a   4. c   5. a   6. c

5 Working with Measurements

1. 80.45
2. 1,000
3. 39.37 inches
4. 0
5. 32
6. Gabriel Daniel Fahrenheit
7. Germany
8. 1686-1736

6 Homonyms

1. add, ad
2. lessen, lesson
3. Shoot, chute
4. aid, aide
5. horse, hoarse
6. fowl, foul
7. butt, but
8. vary, very
9. bawl, ball
10. weekly, weakly
11. fir, fur
12. sheer, shear
13. plum, plumb
14. sense, cents, scents
15. cite, sight, site

Lesson 16

1 Definitions

1. lymph
2. phosphorus
3. asphalt
4. phobia
5. prophecy
6. saxophone
7. pamphlet
8. amphibian
9. pheasant
10. dolphin
11. graphic
12. philosophy
13. autobiography
14. decipher
15. triumph

2 Understanding the Story

1. c   3. b   5. c   7. b   9. b
2. d   4. a   6. b   8. a

3 What Do You Think?

1. Answers will vary. Johnsy probably would have expressed remorse and guilt.
2. Schatz was very tense and probably afraid of dying. He really didn't want to die. Johnsy was tired of trying to stay alive and was willing to let death take her. She didn't appear to fear death.
3. Schatz was filled with disbelief at first (as was Fyodor in "The Execution"). As he realized he wasn't going to die, he began to relax. Johnsy realized that giving up was wrong, and she began to eat and try to get better. She regained hope and started to make plans for the future.

4 Hyphenated Words

1. all-round
2. down-to-earth
3. well-built
4. thick-skinned
5. bird's-eye
6. absent-minded
7. self-conscious
8. full-fledged
9. tongue-in-cheek
10. self-critical
11. high-strung
12. red-handed
13. two-faced
14. hunky-dory
15. far-reaching

5 The $24 Swindle

unsettling
official, colonies, particularly, colony
purchase, claim
intelligent, outright
rival, quibble, chuckling
settled, absolutely, betrayed, situation

Review: Lessons 1-16

1 Word Review

1. a	5. b	9. b	13. d
2. c	6. c	10. c	14. a
3. d	7. b	11. a	15. a
4. b	8. d	12. a	16. c

2 Word Review

1. penguin — bird
2. bigot — enraged
3. mechanical — electrical
4. beagle — hound
5. coarseness — embarrassed
6. jaundiced — brilliance
7. narcotics — menace
8. conceive — unpleasant
9. protective — tragedies
10. parade — majestic
11. hardheaded — cement
12. analysis — cynical

3 Word Sound Review

1. godliness
2. halter
3. Polish
4. powder
5. thaw
6. hyena
7. vocal
8. jaguar
9. reception
10. residue
11. heyday
12. symbol

4 Find the Homonym

isle   chord   soar
bans   doe   tents
beet   jeans   we'd
Cokes   scene   yolk

1. chord
2. we'd
3. doe
4. scene
5. beet
6. isle
7. bans
8. jeans
9. Cokes
10. tents
11. yolk
12. soar

5 A Poet's View of Dying

1. Death is something to be fought and resisted. The speaker doesn't want to die; she will cling vehemently to life. Accept any of the various phrases as evidence.
2. Answers will vary. Accept any reasonable responses.

Lesson 17

1 Definitions

1. khaki
2. rhinestone
3. wreath
4. gherkin
5. knoll
6. ghoul
7. salve
8. porridge
9. wretched
10. ghastly
11. Wright
12. bustle
13. jostle
14. wrangle
15. abridge
16. rustle

2 Understanding the Folktales

1. He thinks he will be rich for the rest of his life.
2. Because he was so used to wishing for things he didn't have, he expressed his thoughts as wishes and used them up foolishly.
3. He doesn't recognize his luck even when it is pointed out to him (the pot of gold under the tree and the maiden).
4. Both wish for riches and lives with fewer hardships, and both foolishly misuse their opportunities when they are given to them.
5. Answers will vary. Accept any reasonable response.

What do you think? Answers will vary. Responses should include the concept that both main characters failed to take advantage of opportunities granted to them.

3 Character Descriptions

1. wrangling
2. prudent
3. courageous
4. moronic
5. ghastly
6. weary
7. heartbroken
8. humble
9. bustling
10. sovereign
11. innocent
12. God-fearing
13. sly
14. boastful
15. bewitched

4 Occupations

Playwrights	**Poets**
acts	rhyme
casts	rhythm
dialogue	stanzas
scenery	verse

Biographers	**Sportswriters**
chapters	headlines
dates	play-offs
diaries	scores
personal letters	trades

5 More about Armenia

invaded, distinct, religion, translated, university
control
World War I, murdered, fled

Soviet, remainder
region, square
farm, manufactured, instruments

6 More about Black Pudding

9, 3, 6, 1, 4, 8, 5, 7, 2

Lesson 18

1 Definitions

1. motto	7. asset	13. essence
2. eddy	8. giddy	14. Sabbath
3. burrow	9. fodder	15. pollute
4. essay	10. rubbish	16. shimmer
5. jimmy	11. commerce	
6. nugget	12. summit	

2 Understanding the Reading

1. c	3. c	5. c	7. b	9. d
2. a	4. b	6. d	8. a	

3 What Do You Think?

1. The characters in both of the folktales pursue the *having* mode of existence because they think that having material wealth will bring them happiness. They are essentially self-centered, and this contributes to their downfall in both cases.
2. Answers will vary. Accept any reasonable response.
3. Answers will vary. Accept any reasonable response.

4 Word Relationships

1. stanza is to ballad
2. tiger is to Asia
3. entangled is to entwined
4. Wilmington is to Delaware
5. mansion is to shack
6. badger is to pester
7. synagogue is to rabbi
8. rookie is to green
9. salve is to medicine
10. busybody is to meddlesome

5 On Latin and Language

1. influence, persists, calculated, roots
2. Romance, derived, tongue, ancient
3. Hemisphere, independent, political, three
4. inscription, buckle, century, B.C.
5. scholars, established, grammar, pour
6. peak, language, throughout, large
7. conquered, unconquered, conquerors, conquer
8. traditional, despite, testify, presence
9. however, exceedingly, translate, translation
10. importance, circumstances, phrases, objects

6 State Search

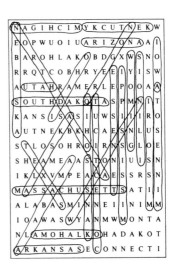

Lesson 19

1 Definitions

1. crimson	6. textile	11. surpass
2. kernel	7. drastic	12. flounder
3. goblin	8. verbal	13. nurture
4. mascot	9. festive	14. plunder
5. ordeal	10. bombard	

2 Understanding the Play

1. They sent very few supplies along with Leslie when he was brought to the Lemkes' from the hospital.
2. Both had been expected to die within a short time. Both needed care that May was willing to give.
3. Dr. Edwards says it is a miracle that the Lemkes have kept Leslie alive for 10 years.
4. May has never given up hope for Leslie even though there has been little progress or improvement in his condition.
5. Leslie has briefly stood alone for the first time.

3 Word Review

1. Rhode Island - smallest
2. biography - abridged
3. bombarded - drastically
4. correct - eyewitnesses
5. burden - burro
6. ego - disinterested
7. bluster - cowering
8. collapsed - ordeal

4 Synonyms and Antonyms

1. confess, deny	7. divine, worldly
2. awesome, humdrum	8. noble, dishonest
3. meddle, ignore	9. random, purposeful
4. blossom, fade	10. fidgety, composed
5. yield, resist	11. comfortable, distressful
6. immortal, temporary	12. wretched, joyous

5 Word Families

1. comfortably	5. moral	9. develop
2. appreciative	6. wretch	10. athlete
3. imprudent	7. immensity	
4. mortal	8. mischievously	

6 Using the Dictionary

Algonquian	French
chipmunk	bureau
possum	chauffeur
raccoon	gourmet
tomahawk	solitaire

German	Spanish
hamburger	burro
kindergarten	chili
sauerkraut	peso
strudel	tornado

Lesson 20

1 Definitions

1. dole
2. dupe
3. vial
4. lure
5. gory
6. null
7. arid
8. tier
9. oral
10. ne'er
11. suet
12. helm
13. mull
14. dote

2 Understanding the Play

1. Sixteen years have passed.
2. The stranger was making fun of Leslie, and May doesn't want Leslie to be the butt of teasing by thoughtless people.
3. When they get a piano for Leslie they discover that he can play any piece of music he hears. Later he begins to sing the words to songs and eventually starts to talk, as well. His musical talent makes him someone to be admired, not teased.
4. It is a person who is generally mentally deficient but who has an exceptional talent or skill in some special area or field. This condition is sometimes referred to as *savant syndrome*.
5. Dr. Vince calls May "amazing" because she has ceaselessly worked to help Leslie and has faith that he will continue to grow and to learn. She believes he will learn to speak someday.

What do you think? Answers will vary. Accept any reasonable response.

3 Which Word Does Not Fit?

1. written
2. Hudson
3. devotion
4. taco
5. Dickens
6. joyous
7. analyze
8. interest
9. Armenia
10. entertain
11. intellectual
12. stop
13. jitters
14. realistic
15. unpopular
16. rhinestone

4 Problems

1. peer pressure
2. injuries
3. inflation
4. calories
5. reality
6. deadlines
7. dandelions
8. dishonesty
9. preservatives
10. jitters
11. ailments
12. posse
13. disobedience
14. spies
15. sharks

5 A Little Latin

1. unicorn
2. unicycle
3. universe
4. uniform
5. biped
6. bifocals
7. bimonthly
8. bisect
9. trimester
10. tripod
11. triangle
12. triceps

6 On Living and Loving: A Poet's Point of View

1. a
2. b
3. c
4. d
5. d
6. a

Review: Lessons 1-20

1 Word Review

1. concerto
2. trestle
3. devotion
4. abide
5. guttural
6. ballad
7. diagonal
8. sect
9. wretch
10. elfin
11. appropriate
12. campus
13. adolescence
14. ego
15. folklore
16. mode

2 Who or What Would You Expect to Be...

1. enthusiastic
2. arid
3. sovereign
4. ancient
5. intellectual
6. abridged
7. rhythmical
8. wee
9. treacherous
10. festive
11. verbal
12. invisible
13. dwindling
14. mischievous
15. unwholesome
16. shimmering

3 A Little More Latin

1. incredible
2. credentials
3. creditor
4. credenza
5. credit
6. credible
7. creed
8. incredibly

4 More Work with Expressions and Proverbs

1. d
2. b
3. b
4. c
5. c
6. a
7. d
8. d
9. b

5 World Capitals

1. Brussels
2. Ottawa
3. Beijing
4. Teheran
5. Baghdad
6. Tokyo
7. Oslo
8. Lisbon
9. Madrid
10. Stockholm
11. Bern
12. Damascus

6 Find the Quote

1. Mercury
2. peppermint
3. kilt
4. Ash Wednesday
5. serial
6. humorous
7. profile
8. hyena
9. coffee
10. poverty
11. wig
12. lemon
13. tuxedo
14. rhythm
15. vitality

A formula for happiness: The way to happiness: keep your heart free from hate, your mind from worry. Live simply. Expect little, give much.

Word Indexes for Book 7

Word Index: Lessons 1–4

A
absent-minded
accidental
acorn
acquire
agreeable
agreeably
allowance
amazement
amazing
anxious
approval
approve
arrange
asset
assignment
awhile

B
bass
behavior
behavioral
being
betray
betrayal
billow
bladder
blazer
blemish
blizzard
blockade
blunder
blunt
bluntly
bravery
brief
briefcase
brilliance
brilliant
brokerage
brutal
brute
burlap
bushel

C
cancel
canoe
carol
cashier
casino
china
China
chum
clan
clarinet
cleanliness
clergy
clique
clotheshorse
comic
compost
Constance
cradle
crayon
credentials
credit
creditor
crock
crocodile
crumble
curious
customary

D
daisy
daughter-in-law
dealership
debtor
deputy
despair
detect
Dickens, C.
disagreeable
disguise
disjoin
disposal
disunity
divide
divorce
doghouse
Dorothy
drab
dragon
drama
dramatic
dribble
drowsy
drudgery
dwindle

E
ebb
effortless
eke
emblem
enrich
equip
erect
Ernie
excitedly
expansion
explosive

F
faithless
fashion
fashionable
favor
fertilize
fiber
finance
financial
financially
fixed
flank
flax
flea-bitten
flimsy
flog
florist
fluster
flutter
fragrance
fragrant
frequent
frequently
frizzy
frosty
frown

G
gene
generosity
generous
generously
glacier
glamorous
glamour
glee
glide
glimmer
glimpse
glint
Gloria
gracious
graciously
graciousness
gratitude
gravity
grid
griddle
grief
gruff
guitar

H
harshly
helplessly
hemp
hers
hissingly
holding
horny
hub
humble
humdrum
humorist
hurricane
hurriedly

I
identify
idleness
Ike
imp
impede
inflict
instantly
instructional
intention
intentional
intersection
inwardly

J
Jerry
Judas
judgmental
Judy
juggle
jute

K
kindle

L
labor
Las Vegas
laughable
Leslie
liable
lilac
lightweight
lilt
loving

M
maple
Maxwell
maze
mechanic
mechanical
melody
mentally
messenger
midst
miller
moneylender
mortgage
motionless
Mozart
muss
mustache

N
nationwide
neighborly
network
Nevada
newly
newscaster
noble
nuclear
nucleus

O
odor
oneness
option
ordinary
oval
overly

P
parole
pastor
pastry
pasture
pathway
patrol
pedal
penitentiary
Pilgrim
pixie
pizza
plaid
plasma
playful
plaza
plod
plumb
plush
Pluto
Plymouth
pointed
possibility
possibly
precious
precision
predicament
prescription
presence
privilege
prizefighter
profound
prolong
proposal
propose
prude
pulp
pulpwood
puny

Q
quake
queerly
quiver

R
rating
recklessly
redbud
redwood
reflection
refusal
region
regional
reptile
R.F.D.
rheumatism
riot
rival
roadway
romance
romp
rove
rumor

S
sane
sap
satisfaction
satisfactory
satisfy
scrawny
scrimmage
scrimp
Scrooge
secretary
senator
senior
shambles
sheen
sheriff
showgirl
shrapnel
shrew
shrewd
shrewdly
shrewdness
shrinkage
shroud
silkily
single-breasted

smolder
snowfall
Sonny
southeastern
splat
splay
splendor
splice
split-level
sprayer
spree
sprightly
sprinkler
sprite
sprocket
spry
stammer
stockholder
straddle
strategy
stricken
strife
strudel
strum
strychnine
subdivision
suburb
subscribe
subscription
sunnily
supposedly
syrup

T
taxpayer
temple
thermos
threesome
threshold
thrice
thrive
throaty
throng
ticker
tiger
tint
topple
tornado
tot
tote
transact
transaction
tremble
tremendous
trial
triple
trombone

trustworthy
tulip

U
umbrella
uncoil
unfashionable
unify
uninteresting
unity
unjust
unknowingly
unmoving
unselfish
upgrade

V
vicious
violin

W
waffle
Walt
wicked
wickedly
wickedness
wide-eyed
widen
willow
workout
woven
Wyoming

X

Y
yen

Z
zest
zesty
zombie

Word Index: Lessons 5-8

A
absence
absorbent
accidentally
acquaint
acquaintance
aide
aimless
aimlessly
Albert
alert
Alexander

Alfred
anxiously
apologetic
apologize
apology
arch
armored
Ash Wednesday
assurance
assure
astonish
auction
auditorium
Australia
Austria
axlike

B
bather
beacon
beetle
beforehand
Bell, A. G.
bewilder
bicker
bloat
bluster
bossily
bothersome
boulevard
broadcast
broadly

C
candidate
carcass
castle
casual
casually
Central America
chandelier
characteristic
charity
Charlotte
chauffeur
chemistry
Cheyenne
chiefly
chiffon
Chile
chili
choir
chophouse
chord
chorus
Christina
Christine
chromium

chromosome
chronological
chute
clasp
cleaver
clergyman
coax
Columbus Day
Commonwealth
Communist
competence
competent
conference
consult
contempt
continent
conversation
crisply

D
Danes
decency
decline
decree
defendant
demonstrate
Denmark
deprive
descend
descendant
determination
determine
determined
develop
devour
dignity
disfigure
disloyal
disloyally
disloyalty
disrespect
doe
dreary
dud
dwarf
dwell
dwelling
Dwight

E
Earl
earnest
earnestly
earnestness
eavesdrop
edition
educational

eh
embarrass
encounter
encouragingly
equipment
era
establish
ether
evident
evidently
examination
extraordinarily
extraordinary

F
failure
familiar
familiarity
fancily
fatherly
feeble
filth
filthy
Finland
fixture
foe
footnote
fortress
Foster, S.
foundation
founder
fragment
furious
furiously

G
Garfield, J.
gasoline
Gene
goalie
Graham
grammar
grimly

H
haggard
Haiti
Harry
hastily
hasty
hatchet
haywire
headlong
hearsay
heed
Herbert

hoe
hoe-down
holly
homestead
hoodlum
Hoover, H.
Howard
howl
humanly
hungrily
hunting
husk
husky

I
Iceland
icepick
idly
incident
incline
incompetent
incomplete
indignant
indignantly
indignation
insanely
insignia
instructive
investigator
it'll

J
jolly
journey

K
kindergarten

L
Labor Day
landscape
landslide
lapse
larder
Laurie
legislation
linger
loam
loiter
lunchroom

M
machine gun
machinist
maim
maintain
Mandy

manufacture
Marian
marvelous
meanness
memorial
Memorial Day
merchant
merely
microscope
Middle Ages
Milky Way
mistletoe
mistress
moat
monument
morn
motherly
mountainside
muzzle

N

nastily
naughtily
naval
neutral
Newton, I.
New Zealand
northerner
nursery

O

observation
observe
observer
occasional
official
officially
oink
Okefenokee
orchestra
orchid
ordinarily
oversize

P

Pa
panther
parched
patrolman
peeve
Pershing, J.
Peru
petticoat
physically
pigment
poinsettia

pointblank
poolroom
prayerfully
precaution
prejudice
prelude
primly
probable
proceed
professor
profile
provision
PTA
purpose

Q

quarrel
queasy
quest

R

ramshackle
random
rapid
red-handed
referee
registration
remembrance
renounce
republic
republican
residence
resident
residential
resign
respectable
responsibly
restlessly
retail
robin

S

sauna
scamper
scan
Scandinavia
scenery
scenic
scent
schedule
scholar
scholarly
scholarship
scissors
scooter
scope
Scranton

scurry
seesaw
select
self-conscious
self-control
self-important
self-respect
sensation
sergeant
shadow
shakily
shanty
shawl
shepherd
shield
shiftless
shun
sickening
silliness
sirloin
skeleton
skimpy
skirmish
slab
slacken
slender
slink
sliver
slogan
slugfest
smashup
smattering
smidgen
smithereens
smug
smugly
sneer
snicker
sniffle
snoop
snug
snuggle
southeast
soybean
Spanish
spatula
spectacles
spectator
speedometer
spinach
spiritual
spiritually
squabble
squadron
squat
squatter
squiggle

squire
stable
stainless
stampede
steadfast
Stephen
stereo
stockily
stocky
stung
sturdily
sturdy
suburban
Suwannee
swab
swagger
swan
Swanee
swap
Swedish
swine
Switzerland
swoop
Sylvia

T

teamster
telegram
telescope
theory
thermometer
thine
thoroughfare
thou
thousandth
thriftily
thy
thyroid
thyself
topcoat
toughness
traditionally
transplant
treacherous
treachery
treasury
troublemaker
tusk
tuxedo
tweak
twelfth
twerp
twiddle
twilight
twinkle

U

unaccented

unacquainted
understanding
undetermined
unfamiliar
unofficial
unsettling
unsightly
untidy
unwisely
usage
utterly

V

Veterans Day

W

Warner
wasp
waterfall
wayfarer
weakly
wee
whew
whimper
whinny
whirlwind
whisk
whiskers
wholesale
wholesome
wildlife
wisp
woe
woodwind
World War I
worrisome

X

Y

yonder

Z

**Word Index:
Lessons 9-12**

A

accuse
achieve
achievement
adjourn
adore
Afghanistan
agony
Alps
alternate

altogether
announcer
Aphrodite
apparent
apparently
Ares
ark
Arkansas
armor
arouse
arrangement
arrogance
article
astonishment
Athena
atom
atomic
auctioneer
avenge
awe
awkward

B

balance
bamboo
bandit
bargain
barnyard
basically
bayou
beige
bellow
bemoan
beware
birdlike
bleary
bluntness
boar
bog
boldly
bolster
brawl
bristle
browse
bruiser
Buddhism
Buddhist
bulldozer

C

callous
cannibal
cardinal
carefree
Carol
casualness
cello

cemetery
China Sea
Chinese
circuit
circular
civilization
coarse
coarsely
coaxingly
cobra
companion
comparison
conceited
conceive
constant
corridor
coupon
courteous
courteously
courtesy
courtship
courtyard
crafty
critical
crumple
culprit
cultivate
cultivated
cushion
Cyclops

D
deafen
dealing
deceive
Delaware
deliberate
deliberately
delicatessen
demon
dew
dike
dismal
distinct
distinctly
doubtless
douse
drowsiness

E
earthen
earthy
eave
eerie
elevator
encircle
enclose

endear
endearment
endorse
enfold
establishment
eternal
eternity
evenly

F
fair-haired
feebleness
fiercely
floodgate
flourish
folly
foolishness
fortunate
fortunately
fowl
freighter
full-fledged
furnace

G
garment
Gary
godliness
gourd
gourmet
grassland
grayish
grievance
grieve

H
Hades
halfway
halter
hearse
heave
Hebrew
helping
hemisphere
Hermes
hermit
hesitate
Highlands
hoarse
hoarsely
Homer
hoop
horizon
horrible
hostess
huddle
hygiene

I
impair
India
inert
informer
instill
intelligently
interrupt
irk
irksome
Ithaca

J
jabber
jilt
jokingly
jolt
journal

K
Kabul
kangaroo
kilt
kingdom

L
lair
lazily
leer
lessen
lurk

M
Mercury
mere
mildew
millionaire
Minerva
misfortune
missile
mole
motive
mourn
mournful
mournfully
mourning
mushroom
mysteriously

N
narcotic
neigh
Neptune
New Mexico
Noah
nomination

nourish
nourishment
nuisance

O
obligation
Odysseus
odyssey
offense
olive
oneself
openly
oppose
Oregon
oust
outpouring

P
paragraph
pebble
peerless
perceive
persuade
persuasion
persuasive
peso
pew
physicist
pioneer
plaster
pleat
polish
Polish
pony
populate
Poseidon
prairie
precede
prevention
proceeding
prophesy
prosper
proverb
provider
pull-up
pulpy
pulpit
pumpkin
purgatory
pursue
pursuit

Q
queasiness
quitter

R
raccoon

recruit
regulate
rehearsal
rehearse
reign
reindeer
relish
remainder
remarry
removal
residue
resource
retaliation
revenge
revenue
Roman
romantic
rouble
rouge
roulette
rural

S
sadden
sardine
Saturn
savage
savagely
scornfulness
Scottish
scoundrel
scow
scrawniness
seize
seizure
severe
severely
shear
shears
shrilly
siege
silently
sincere
sincerely
sincerity
sizzle
skimpiness
sluice
solitaire
soupy
South American
Southerner
souvenir
sphere
spat
spouse
steward

stewardess
stowaway
sturdiness
subdue
suddenness
suitable
suitably
sunbeam
super
swarthy
swerve
swindler
sword

T
tablet
temporarily
text
threadbare
thriftiness
tiresome
tomahawk
topic
torture
totality
tour
tourist
tournament
tourniquet
tow
tower
traditional
Trojan War
trolley
trot
trowel
Troy
Truman, H.
typhoon

U
unachieved
unapparent
unbearably
unfortunate
unfortunately
unintentional
unlatch
unmatched
unnourishing
unrehearsed
unsuitable
unto
untouched
unwillingly
uphold
upright
urban

penguin
percussion
permanent
pharmacist
pheasant
Philippines
philosopher
philosophy
phobia
Phoenix
phooey
phosphorus
photographic
pianist
pigeon
pneumonia
poop
postage
praiseworthy
prediction
preparation
principal
procession
proclaim
professional
prophecy
protective
psalm
purgative
purposeless
pygmy
Pyle, H.
python

Q
quail
quaint
quibble
quicken

R
ragtime
Randolph
reception
receptionist
rectangle
reddish
rookie
Rudolph

S
salamander
saxophone
scaffold
seaworthy
self-addressed

self-critical
self-evident
self-seeking
sensible
sentry
sewage
shorn
Sicily
similar
single-minded
site
slither
smart aleck
snout
Sophia
Sophie
sophomore
specially
spigot
springy
starry-eyed
straggle
studio
submerge
supporter
surgeon
surgery
switchboard
sycamore
Sydney
sympathetic
sympathy
symphony
synagogue
Syracuse
Syria
syringe

T
technical
tempo
terrific
thick-skinned
thin-skinned
tongue-in-cheek
tonic
tragedy
tragically
treacherously
triangle
triumph
triumphant
triumphantly
trod
troublesome
two-faced
tzar

U
unauthorized
unbound
understandable
unsteadily
upturned
urine

V
vacuum
varnish
vocal
vogue

W
waddle
wag
waggle
warmhearted
wart
waterway
waylay
wearily
weariness
well-balanced
well-built
well-fed
who'd
Wilmington
windowpane
wishfully
withstand
workroom
wreckage
wrongdoing

X
xylophone

Y
yellow-bellied

Z
zinc

Word Index: Lessons 17-20

A
abide
ably
abridge
absorb
acceptable
accompany
actively

addict
adolescence
adolescent
alas
album
ale
alto
ancient
anew
appreciate
appreciation
appreciative
appropriate
arid
Armenia
Armenian
artistic
assent
assert
athlete
athletic
athletics
atlas
attentively
awaken
awesome
awkwardly

B
babe
Bach, J. S.
bade
badger
Baghdad
ballad
Beijing
Belgium
Bern
bewitch
bias
bifocals
Bill
bimonthly
biped
bisect
blister
blossom
bombard
boredom
briefly
Brussels
buckle
bundle
burr
burro
burrow
bustle
butler

C
campus
capsize
carp
cartridge
cerebral palsy
challenge
characterize
Cheddar
chipmunk
Chopin, F.
chowder
coldness
collapse
collection
collide
collision
comfortable
comfortably
commerce
communication
concerto
condense
connection
conquer
conquerable
conqueror
considerable
constantly
contrary
cordon
corsage
counselor
courageous
cower
crave
credenza
credible
crimson
croon
crosspiece
cult
cutthroat
cynically

D
Damascus
dandelion
dangle
dazzle
deathlike
decoration
defy
demonstrator
densely
deny
destructive

development
devotion
diagonal
diagonally
diaper
dishonesty
disinterested
dole
dote
Douglas
drastic
drastically
drum majorette
dual
dupe

E
eddy
educate
effective
ego
elder
elfin
empire
enchant
endanger
enliven
enslave
entangle
enthusiastic
entrust
entwine
epic
erupt
escort
essay
essence
exceedingly
expressionless
eyeglasses
eyewitness

F
fair-minded
fairylike
Fanny
feeble-minded
festival
festive
fidget
finely
flounder
fodder
folklore
formula
framework
furrow

Word Index: Lessons 1-20

A

abide
ably
abnormal
abnormally
abridge
absence
absent-minded
absolute
absolutely
absorb
absorbent
acceptable
accidental
accidentally
accompany
accuse
achieve
achievement
acorn
acquaint
acquaintance
acquire
actively
addict
adjourn
adolescence
adolescent
Adolphe
adore
Afghanistan
agenda
agony
agreeable
agreeably
aide
aimless
aimlessly
alas
Albert
album
ale
alert
Alexander
Alfred
allowance
all-round
almond
Alps
alternate
alto
altogether
amazement
amazing
amphibian
analysis
analyze
ancient
anew
angina
angle
announcer
anxious
anxiously
Aphrodite
apologetic
apologize
apology
apparent
apparently
appreciate
appreciation
appreciative
appropriate
approval
approve
arch
Ares
arid
ark
Arkansas
Armenia
Armenian
armor
armored
arouse
arrange
arrangement
arrogance
article
artistic
Ash Wednesday
asphalt
assent
assert
asset
assignment
assurance
assure
astonish
astonishment
Athena
athlete
athletic
athletics
atlas
atom
atomic
attentively
auction
auctioneer
auditorium
Australia
Austria

B

babe
Bach, J. S.
bade
badger
badminton
Baghdad
balance
balcony
ballad
bamboo
bandage
bandit
bargain
barnyard
baseman
basically
bass
bather
bayonet
bayou
beacon
beagle
beaklike
bedside
bedstead
beetle
beforehand
behavior
behavioral
beige
Beijing
being
Belgium
Bell, A. G.
bellow
bemoan
Bern
betray
betrayal
beverage
beware
bewilder
bewitch
bias

autobiographical
autobiography
autograph
avenge
awaken
awe
awesome
awhile
awkward
awkwardly
axlike

bicker
bifocals
bigot
Bill
billow
bimonthly
biographer
biographical
biography
biped
birdlike
bird's-eye
bisect
bladder
blazer
bleary
blemish
blister
blizzard
bloat
blockade
blossom
bluish
blunder
blunt
bluntly
bluntness
bluster
boar
bog
boldly
bolster
bombard
boredom
bossily
bothersome
boulevard
brainstorm
bravery
brawl
brief
briefcase
briefly
brilliance
brilliant
brilliantly
bristle
British Isles
broadcast
broadly
brokerage
browse
bruiser
Brussels
brutal
brute
buckle

Buddhism
Buddhist
buffalo
bulldozer
bundle
bureau
burlap
burr
burro
burrow
bushel
bustle
butler
butt
bygone
bylaw

C

cabinetwork
cable
cafeteria
calculate
calculation
calculator
callous
callousness
campus
canal
cancel
candidate
cannibal
canoe
capsize
carcass
cardinal
carefree
carnival
carob
Carol
carol
carp
cartridge
cashier
casino
castle
casual
casually
casualness
casualty
cavity
cedar
celebration
celebrity
celery
cello
cement
cemetery

censor
censorship
centigrade
Central America
cerebral palsy
ceremony
challenge
chandelier
characteristic
characterize
charade
charity
Charlotte
chauffeur
Cheddar
chemist
chemistry
Cheyenne
chicken-hearted
chiefly
chiffon
Chile
chili
china
China
China Sea
Chinese
chipmunk
choir
chophouse
Chopin, F.
chord
chorus
chowder
Christina
Christine
chromium
chromosome
chronological
chum
chute
cipher
circuit
circular
citrus
civil
civilian
civilization
clan
clank
clarinet
clasp
cleanliness
cleaver
clergy
clergyman
clique

cloak
clotheshorse
coarse
coarsely
coarseness
coax
coaxingly
cobra
coldness
collapse
collection
collide
collision
Columbus Day
column
columnist
comedy
come-on
comfortable
comfortably
comic
commence
commerce
Commonwealth
communication
Communist
companion
comparison
competence
competent
compost
conceited
conceive
concerto
condemn
condense
conference
confrontation
connection
conquer
conquerable
conqueror
consequence
considerable
Constance
constant
constantly
consult
contempt
continent
contrary
conversation
cordon
correction
corridor
corsage
cottage

counselor
counterfeit
coupon
courageous
courteous
courteously
courtesy
courtship
courtyard
covey
cower
cradle
crafty
crave
crayon
credentials
credenza
credible
credit
creditor
crimson
crisply
critical
crock
crocodile
croon
crosspiece
crucifix
crumble
crumple
crystal
cuckoo
culprit
cult
cultivate
cultivated
curious
cushion
customary
cutthroat
Cyclops
cylinder
cymbal
cynical
cynically
Cynthia
cypress

D

daisy
Damascus
dandelion
Danes
dangle
Daniel
daughter-in-law
dazzle

deafen
dealership
dealing
deathlike
debtor
deceive
decency
decipher
decline
decode
decoration
decree
defendant
defy
degrade
Delaware
delay
deliberate
deliberately
delicatessen
demon
demonstrate
demonstrator
Denmark
densely
deny
deprive
deputy
derive
descend
descendant
despair
destructive
detect
determination
determine
determined
develop
development
devotion
devour
dew
diagonal
diagonally
diaper
Dickens, C.
dignity
dike
dimly
disagreeable
disciple
discipline
disfigure
disguise
dishearten
dishonesty
disinterested

disjoin
disloyal
disloyally
disloyalty
dismal
disposal
disrespect
distinct
distinctly
disunity
divide
divine
divorce
doe
doghouse
dole
dolphin
Dorothy
Dostoyevsky, F.
dote
doubtless
Douglas
douse
downstage
drab
draggle
dragon
drama
dramatic
drastic
drastically
drawer
dreary
dribble
drowsiness
drowsy
drudgery
drum majorette
dual
dud
dupe
dwarf
dwell
dwelling
Dwight
dwindle
dynasty

E

eagle
Earl
earnest
earnestly
earnestness
earthen
earthy
eave

eavesdrop
ebb
ebony
eddy
edition
editor
educate
educational
eerie
effective
effortless
ego
eh
eke
elder
electrical
elevator
elfin
embarrass
embarrassment
emblem
empire
encamp
encase
enchant
encircle
enclose
encounter
encouragingly
endanger
endear
endearment
endorse
energetic
energetically
enfold
enliven
enrage
enrich
enslave
entangle
enthusiastic
entrust
entwine
epic
epidemic
equip
equipment
era
erect
Ernie
erupt
escort
essay
essence
establish
establishment

eternal
eternity
Ethel
ether
European
evenly
evident
evidently
evolve
examination
exceedingly
excerpt
excitedly
execute
execution
exit
expansion
explosive
expressionless
extraordinarily
extraordinary
eyeglasses
eyewitness

F

fabric
Fahrenheit
failure
fair-haired
fair-minded
fairylike
faithless
familiar
familiarity
fancily
Fanny
far-off
far-out
far-sighted
fashion
fashionable
fatherly
fatigue
favor
feeble
feeble-minded
feebleness
fertilize
fertilizer
festival
festive
fiber
fidget
fiercely
filth
filthy
finance

financial
financially
finely
Finland
fixed
fixture
flank
flax
flea-bitten
flimsy
flog
floodgate
florist
flounder
flourish
Floyd
fluster
flutter
fodder
foe
folklore
folly
foolishness
footnote
forbidden
formula
fortress
fortunate
fortunately
fortuneteller
Foster, S.
foundation
founder
fowl
foyer
fragment
fragrance
fragrant
framework
frankly
freighter
frequent
frequently
frizzy
frosty
frown
full-bodied
full-dress
full-fashioned
full-fledged
fungus
furious
furiously
furnace
furrow
Fyodor

G

Gabriel
gaggle
gal
galaxy
gangrene
Garfield, J.
garment
Gary
gasoline
gel
gelatin
gene
Gene
generator
generosity
generous
generously
genius
genuine
geyser
ghastly
gherkin
ghetto
ghostly
ghoul
ghoulish
giddy
glacier
Gladys
glamorous
glamour
glassy
glee
glide
glimmer
glimpse
glint
Gloria
goalie
goblin
God-fearing
godliness
good-for-nothing
goodly
gory
Gospel
gourd
gourmet
gracious
graciously
graciousness
Graham
grammar
graphic
graphite
grassland
gratitude

gravity
grayish
Greenwich
gremlin
grid
griddle
grief
grievance
grieve
grimace
grimly
gruff
guidance
guilder
guitar
guttural
gymnastic

H
Hades
haggard
haggle
Haiti
halfway
hallway
halter
haltingly
hand-to-mouth
hanky-panky
happy-go-lucky
hardheaded
Harry
harshly
hastily
hasty
hatchet
haywire
headlong
headpiece
hearsay
hearse
heartbroken
heave
Hebrew
hedge
heed
heighten
helm
helping
helplessly
helter-skelter
he-man
hemisphere
hemp
Herbert
Hermes
hermit

hers
hesitate
heyday
hiccups
Highlands
high-minded
high-pitched
high-sounding
high-strung
hinder
hissingly
hit-or-miss
hoarse
hoarsely
hoe
hoe-down
holding
holly
Homer
homestead
homeward
hoodlum
hoop
Hoover, H.
hopefully
hopelessly
horizon
horizontal
horny
horrible
horrid
hostage
hostess
Howard
howl
hub
hubbub
huddle
Hudson
humanly
humble
humdrum
humiliate
humiliation
humorist
Humphrey
hungrily
hunky-dory
hunting
hurdle
hurdy-gurdy
hurricane
hurriedly
husk
husky
hustle
hustler

hydrogen
hyena
hygiene
hyphen
hyphenate
hypnosis
hypnotist
hypnotize
hypocrite
hysteria
hysterical

I
iceberg
Iceland
icepick
icily
Idaho
identify
identity
idiot
idiot savant
idleness
idly
idol
Ike
illogical
immensely
immensity
immoral
immorality
immortal
immortality
imp
impair
impede
imprudent
incident
incline
incompetent
incomplete
incredible
incredibly
India
indignant
indignantly
indignation
indirectly
inert
infant
inflict
influenza
informer
insanely
insanity
inscription
insecurely

insignia
instantly
instill
instructional
instructive
intellectual
intelligently
intention
intentional
interrupt
intersection
investigator
invisible
inwardly
iodine
Iran
Iraq
irk
irksome
isle
Ithaca
it'll

J
jabber
Jacob
jaguar
janitor
jaundice
Jenny
Jerry
jilt
jimmy
jitters
jittery
JoAnna
jokingly
jolly
jolt
Joseph
Josephine
jostle
journal
journey
joyous
Judas
judgmental
Judy
juggle
jumble
Jupiter
jute

K
Kabul
kangaroo
Kansas

Kentucky
kernel
khaki
kilometer
kilt
kindergarten
kindle
kingdom
knave
knighthood
knoll
know-it-all
knowledgeable
Knoxville

L
labor
Labor Day
lad
lair
landscape
landslide
lap dog
lapse
larceny
larder
lasagna
Las Vegas
Latin
Latin America
laughable
Laurie
lava
lavatory
lawless
lazily
leadership
lecture
leer
legend
leggings
legislation
Leslie
lessen
liable
liar
lifeless
lightweight
lilac
lilt
lily-livered
Lima
lima bean
linger
Lisbon
Lloyd
loam

logic
logical
loiter
loving
lulu
lunchroom
lure
lurk
lymph

M
machine gun
machinist
madness
Madrid
magnet
maiden
maim
maintain
majestic
majesty
malice
mallet
Mandy
manufacture
maple
margarine
Marian
marigold
marvelous
mascot
matter-of-fact
maturity
Maxwell
maze
McDonald
mealy-mouthed
meanness
mechanic
mechanical
meddle
meddlesome
melody
memo
memorial
Memorial Day
menace
mentally
merchant
Mercury
mercury
mere
merely
messenger
microscope
Middle Ages
midget

midst
mildew
mileage
Milky Way
miller
millionaire
mimic
Minerva
mingle
Minnesota
minnow
Minuit, P.
minus
mischief
mischievous
mischievously
miserable
misfortune
missile
mistletoe
mistress
moat
mode
model
moisture
mole
moneylender
Monopoly
monument
morality
morbid
morgue
morn
moron
moronic
mortal
mortality
mortgage
Moslem
motherly
motionless
motive
motto
mountainous
mountainside
mourn
mournful
mournfully
mourning
mover
Mozart
mull
mum
mushroom
musician
musket

muss
mustache
muzzle
mysteriously

N
Naples
narcotic
narrate
narrator
nastily
nationwide
naturalist
naughtily
naval
Nebraska
ne'er
ne'er-do-well
neigh
neighborly
Neptune
nestle
network
neutral
Nevada
newborn
newly
New Mexico
newscaster
New South Wales
Newton, I.
New Zealand
Nicholas
Nichols
nightstick
Noah
noble
nobleman
Noel
nomination
nonstop
North Dakota
northerner
noteworthy
noticeable
nourish
nourishment
nuclear
nucleus
nugget
nuisance
null
nursery
nurture
nutritionist
nymph

O
obligation
oboe
observation
observe
observer
occasional
odor
Odysseus
odyssey
offense
official
officially
offstage
off-the-record
oink
Okefenokee
old-fashioned
Old World
olive
oneness
oneself
onset
onyx
openly
open-minded
opponent
oppose
option
oral
orally
orchestra
orchid
ordeal
ordinarily
ordinary
Oregon
orphan
orphanage
Oslo
Ottawa
oust
outpost
outpouring
outrageous
outrageously
outright
outward
oval
overlap
overly
oversize
overwhelm

P
Pa

palsy
pamper
pamphlet
pansy
panther
parade
paragraph
paralysis
paralyze
parched
Parcheesi
parlor
parole
pastor
pastry
pasture
pathway
patrol
patrolman
peasant
pebble
pedal
peerless
peeve
penguin
penitentiary
pennant
peppermint
perceive
percussion
permanent
Perry
Pershing, J.
personality
persuade
persuasion
persuasive
Peru
peso
petticoat
pew
pharmacist
pheasant
Philippines
philosopher
philosophy
phobia
Phoenix
phooey
phosphorus
photographic
physically
physicist
pianist
pigeon
pigment
Pilgrim

pioneer
pistol
piston
pixie
pizza
plaid
plasma
plaster
play-off
playful
playwright
plaza
pleat
plod
plumb
plunder
plush
Pluto
Plymouth
pneumonia
poetry
poinsettia
pointblank
pointed
polish
Polish
pollute
pony
poolroom
poop
populate
porpoise
porridge
Portugal
Portuguese
Poseidon
posse
possibility
possibly
possum
postage
posy
prairie
praiseworthy
prayerfully
precaution
precede
precious
precision
predicament
prediction
prejudice
prelude
premature
preparation
prescription
presence

prevention
primly
principal
privilege
prizefighter
probable
proceed
proceeding
procession
proclaim
professional
professor
profile
profound
prolong
pronounce
prophecy
prophesy
proposal
propose
prosper
protective
protectively
proverb
provider
provision
prude
prudent
prudently
psalm
PTA
puberty
pull-up
pulp
pulpit
pulpwood
pulpy
pumpkin
puny
purgative
purgatory
purplish
purpose
purposeful
purposeless
pursue
pursuit
pygmy
Pyle, H.
python

Q
quail
quaint
quake
qualify
quarrel

queasiness
queasy
queerly
quest
quibble
quicken
quitter
quiver

R
rabbi
raccoon
raffle
ragtime
ramshackle
Randolph
random
rapid
rapture
rating
reception
receptionist
recklessly
recording
recruit
rectangle
redbud
reddish
red-handed
redwood
referee
reflection
refrain
refusal
region
regional
registration
regulate
rehearsal
rehearse
reign
reindeer
relish
rely
remainder
remarry
remembrance
removal
renounce
repetition
reptile
republic
republican
residence
resident
residential
residue

resign
resist
resource
respectable
responsibly
restlessly
retail
retaliation
retard
retarded
revenge
revenue
revolting
R.F.D.
rhapsody
rheumatism
rhinestone
rhinoceros
Rhode Island
rhythm
rhythmical
ridiculous
riot
ripple
rival
roadway
robin
Roman
romance
Romance
romantic
romp
rookie
rouble
rouge
roulette
rove
rubbish
Rudolph
rummage
rumor
rural
rustle
rustler

S
Sabbath
sacrifice
sadden
salamander
salmon
salve
sane
sap
sardine
satisfaction
satisfactory

satisfy
Saturn
sauna
savage
savagely
saxophone
scaffold
scamper
scan
Scandinavia
scenery
scenic
scent
schedule
scholar
scholarly
scholarship
scissors
scooter
scope
scornfulness
Scottish
scoundrel
scow
Scranton
scrawniness
scrawny
scrimmage
scrimp
Scrooge
scurry
seaworthy
secretary
sect
seesaw
seize
seizure
select
self-addressed
self-centeredness
self-conscious
self-control
self-critical
self-evident
self-important
selfishness
selflessness
self-respect
self-seeking
senator
senior
sensation
sensible
sentry
sequence
sergeant
serial

session
severe
severely
sewage
sewn
shadow
shakily
shambles
shanty
shawl
shear
shears
sheen
shepherd
sheriff
shield
shiftless
shimmer
shimmy
shorn
showgirl
showpiece
shrapnel
shrew
shrewd
shrewdly
shrewdness
shrilly
shrinkage
shroud
shuffle
shun
Sicily
sickening
siege
silently
silkily
silliness
similar
sincere
sincerely
sincerity
single-breasted
single-minded
sirloin
site
sizzle
skeleton
skimpiness
skimpy
skirmish
Skivvies
slab
slacken
slender
slink
slither

sliver
slogan
slugfest
sluice
smart aleck
smashup
smattering
smidgen
smithereens
smolder
smug
smugly
sneer
snicker
sniffle
snoop
snout
snowfall
snug
snuggle
solitaire
solitary
someday
Sonny
Sophia
Sophie
sophomore
soupy
South American
South Dakota
southeast
southeastern
southerner
souvenir
sovereign
soybean
Spanish
spat
spatula
specialist
specially
species
specific
spectacles
spectator
speedometer
sphere
spigot
spinach
spiritual
spiritually
splat
splay
splendor
splice
split-level
sportswriter

spouse
sprayer
spree
sprightly
springy
sprinkler
sprite
sprocket
spry
squabble
squadron
squashy
squat
squatter
squiggle
squire
squishy
stable
stainless
stammer
stampede
stanza
starry-eyed
steadfast
stencil
Stephen
stereo
steward
stewardess
stiffen
stimulate
stimulation
stockholder
Stockholm
stockily
stocky
storyteller
stowaway
straddle
strategy
straggle
stricken
strife
strudel
strum
strychnine
studio
stung
sturdily
sturdiness
sturdy
subdivision
subdue
submerge
subscribe
subscription
suburb

suburban
suddenness
suet
suitable
suitably
summit
sunbeam
sunnily
super
superior
supporter
supposedly
surgeon
surgery
surpass
Suwannee
swab
swagger
swan
Swanee
swap
swarthy
Swedish
swerve
swindler
swine
switchboard
Switzerland
swoop
sword
sycamore
Sydney
Sylvia
sympathetic
sympathy
symphony
synagogue
Syracuse
Syria
syringe
syrup

T
tablet
taco
tallow
taxpayer
Tchaikovsky, P.
teamster
technical
Teheran
telegram
telescope
temple
tempo
temporarily
terrific

text
textbook
textile
theory
thereupon
thermometer
thermos
thick-skinned
thine
thin-skinned
thoroughfare
thou
thousandth
threadbare
threesome
threshold
thrice
thriftily
thriftiness
thrive
throaty
throng
thy
thyroid
thyself
ticker
tidbit
tier
tiger
tiller
tinder
tinsel
tint
tiresome
Tokyo
tomahawk
tongue-in-cheek
tonic
topcoat
topic
topple
tornado
torture
tot
totality
tote
totem
toughness
tour
tourist
tournament
tourniquet
tow
towards
tower
traditional
traditionally

tragedy
tragically
transact
transaction
translate
translation
translator
transplant
treacherous
treacherously
treachery
treasury
tremble
tremendous
trestle
trial
triangle
triceps
trimester
triple
tripod
triumph
triumphant
triumphantly
trod
Trojan War
trolley
trombone
trot
troublemaker
troublesome
trowel
Troy
Truman, H.
trustworthy
tulip
Turkey
Turkish
tusk
tuxedo
tweak
twelfth
twerp
twiddle
twilight
twinkle
two-faced
typhoon
tzar

U
umbrella
unaccented
unaccompanied
unaccustomed
unachieved
unacquainted

unapparent
unauthorized
unbearably
unbound
unchangeable
uncoil
uncomfortable
uncomfortably
unconcerned
unconquered
understandable
understanding
undertake
undetermined
undeveloped
uneducated
unescorted
unfamiliar
unfashionable
unfortunate
unfortunately
unhappiness
unicorn
unicycle
unify
unintentional
uninteresting
unity
unjust
unknowingly
unlatch
unmatched
unmoving
unnourishing
unofficial
unrehearsed
unselfish
unsettling
unsightly
unsteadily
unsuitable
untidy
unto
untouched
unwholesome
unwillingly
unwisely
upgrade
uphold
upright
upturned
urban
urine
usage
utmost
utterly
uttermost

V

vacuum
valve
various
varnish
vary
veer
Venus
verbal
verdict
versus
vertical
Veterans Day
vial
vicious
villain
Vince
violence
violent
violently
violin
virgin
Virginia
virtue
visible
vitality
vocal
vogue
voltage
volume
voodoo
vouch

W

waddle
waffle
wag
waggle
Walt
Wang
warily
warmhearted
Warner
wart
wary
wasp
waterfall
waterway
waver
wayfarer
waylay
weakly
wearily
weariness
weary
wedge
wee

well-balanced
well-built
well-fed
wheelbarrow
whew
whimper
whinny
whirlwind
whisk
whiskers
who'd
wholehearted
wholesale
wholesome
whoops
whosoever
wicked
wickedly
wickedness
wide-eyed
widen
widow
widower
wield
wildlife
willow
Wilmington
windowpane
Wisconsin
wishfully
wisp
withdrawn
withstand
woe
wolf
woodcutter
woodwind
word-of-mouth
workout
workroom
World War I
worrisome
woven
wrangle
wreckage
wretch
wretched
wretchedly
wriggle
Wright
wrongdoing
Wyoming

X

Xmas
xylophone

Y

yacht
yearn
yellow-bellied
Yellow River
yen
yonder

Z

zest
zesty
Zeus
zinc
zombie
zoom